THE COMPLETE COMEDY WRITER

Make your sitcom, stand-up, screenplay, sketches and stories 62% funnier

Dave Cohen

"There are few more experienced comedy writers than Dave Cohen. Take heed of his wise words." Jim Howick

https://www.davecohen.org.uk/

The Complete Comedy Writer

Published by TTTTTT Publications, 2022

ISBN No: 978-1-9993138-7-6

https://www.davecohen.org.uk/

"**Dave Cohen gives great notes.**" Sam Bain, co-writer and creator Peep Show, Fresh Meat, Babylon

"**People say you can't analyse comedy. They're wrong, they mean they can't. Dave Cohen can.**" Gary Delaney

"**Anyone who wants to get into comedy writing should do one of Dave's courses. He's a right laugh and I think there were biscuits.**" Sian Harries, writer Man Down, Here Be Dragons, The Tourist Trap

"**Dave writes about comedy more concisely and in more depth than I ever could. For this reason alone I dislike him intensely.**" Omid Djalili

"**Dave is a highly experienced comedy writer and has written some of the best material on Horrible Histories. He's also a terrific teacher. Not many people know more about the craft.**" Bill Dare, senior tutor NFTS Comedy Writing and Production Course 2014-21, Creator-producer Dead Ringers

"**Engaging, informative and beautifully written**" Tim Dawson, writer, Coming Of Age

"**Awesome notes.**" Ali Cook, comedian, writer, magician, Dirty Tricks (Channel 4)

How To Be Averagely Successful at Comedy (2013)

"**Utterly indispensable guide for anyone wanting to make a living at comedy, and very funny too.**" British Comedy Guide

"**A gag-packed insight into the inner workings of the comedy world. Go out and bloody well buy the whole book.**" Bruce Dessau, Beyond The Joke

"**An engrossing, entertaining read.**" Steve Bennett, Chortle.co.uk

This book is dedicated to Jonny

Contents

Introduction

Writing comedy is one of the weirdest jobs in the world.

I was a stand-up comedian for ten years and that wasn't exactly normal. But at least it was measurable. I stood in a room full of strangers and spoke. As long as I made them laugh out loud six or more times a minute, I was doing well. Three or four times was okay. Anything less meant I wasn't asked back.

Now every morning I get up, stare at a blank piece of paper or screen, and invent sentences or conversations that I hope will make a complete stranger laugh. They might be watching TV or reading a book or listening to the radio. That moment could be months or years away.

I always wanted to be a writer but couldn't take it seriously. When I was ten an English teacher gave me terrible marks and wrote on my school report "he must stop putting jokes in his essays." Years later I became a journalist on a local newspaper and was ticked off by my editor for introducing sarcasm to council meeting reports.

There was only one job I could do, and this was it.

Four years ago, I published the first edition of this book. Wrote about how different things had become since I'd quit the local paper in 1983, and started to earn a living at jesting.

Alternative comedy had exploded onto our TVs and blown away the establishment. Rik Mayall, French and Saunders, Alexei Sayle were the new stars. The BBC had been reliant for decades on a small elite of Oxbridge educated men. Controllers, guardians, and producers of the nation's mirth output, they were struggling to keep up.

I wanted to "do comedy" with only a vague idea of what that meant. Luckily, I moved to London at the exact moment when demand for live entertainment was growing faster than the supply of comedians to present it. You didn't have to be a great performer to make a living as a stand-up.

I wasn't, and did.

I began attending weekly meetings in an anonymous BBC office block, round the corner from Broadcasting House. Tuesday afternoon, four o'clock. You walked in off the street, as anyone was allowed to do, into the Department of Radio Light Entertainment at 16 Langham Street, upstairs to a stuffy room crammed with wannabe comedy writers of every age and odour, but only one gender.

A list of news stories was read out by a man who told us he was the producer of the weekly topical radio show Week Ending. We had 48 hours to write jokes for the programme, which was recorded on Friday morning and broadcast the same night.

Week Ending was a year-round show that was the principal training ground for writers, performers, producers and future heads of comedy. Douglas Adams started there. Armando Iannucci. Rory Bremner. Griff Rhys Jones. David Jason. And little me.

16 Langham Street was demolished 20 years ago, disappearing around the same time as Week Ending, and the BBC's domination of comedy.

In 2018 I noted that we appeared to be in similar rapidly changing times. The streaming and smartphone revolutions had already begun. The idea of everyone sitting down to watch one episode of their favourite TV show at a set time was already vanishing. TikTok was a small but growing platform, already millions were picking up their laughs from YouTube.

Self-publishing was moving from the image of the smug chief executive's vanity book to a business model that could allow anyone to write and publish their own comic novels.

The idea of what was meant by sitcom was in a similar state of flux.

"What's a sitcom?" I asked. "Mrs Brown's Boys? Fleabag? Apparently yes and yes. It's not obvious yet but over the next few years, when this generation that's stopped watching TV shows at specific times grows up to become the one that makes them, we could see a fundamental shift from the models we're used to of big TV stations, channels, and so much else we've taken for granted."

That change was accelerated by covid. Mirroring the growing divide across the world between rich and poor, the streaming companies have devoured most of the budgets that had previously gone to smaller players like the BBC. Even the larger comedy companies like Talkback have been swallowed by giant global media corporations. Online humour, made for a budget of 50p, has mushroomed.

In 2022, it's never been harder to get past the gatekeepers and into the professional world of comedy creation. And it's never been easier to write, create, edit and promote your own.

I can't teach you how to be funny. If you think you are, then I can help you find a quicker way to the jokes. Are you already achieving some success as a comedy writer? I can help you focus on the characters and stories that drive your scripts. Point you in the right direction to accelerate your career.

I can't tell you how to write your stories. I can make suggestions based on things that have worked for me. Have several decades of mistakes to recall, and advice on how to avoid them. I wouldn't presume to call myself a teacher.

Think of me as a Human Signpost.

In Part One, we spend lots of time inside your head. Think of an idea, imagine it's your favourite show, movie or novel and work out why you like it so much.

In Parts Two and Three, we start to develop your characters and stories.

Part Four is for what you write: dialogue, complications, conflict and jokes. Lots of jokes. Lots to find out about how to write them.

Part Five is all about rewriting.

In Part Six we investigate other ways to proactively develop your comedy writing career.

Four years ago, in the first edition, I pointed out that some things were the same.

"35 years since I turned up for those weekly topical comedy meetings, when everything was changing and uncertain in the world of comedy, it's still possible to start your comedy career writing jokes and sketches for BBC Radio. You can't walk in off the street anymore, which is definitely a good thing, but you can begin getting your work broadcast fairly quickly.

You can still meet new writers and producers, hook up with them and push your ideas. You can still go to the Edinburgh Fringe.

And even if you don't manage to get your work broadcast, you can sell your jokes on the internet. Or give them away on Twitter, which is not so great but plenty of people earn a living from gag writing thanks to starting out there."

Four years ago, I was writing mostly about comedy on radio and TV. Sitcom, topical, sketches. And they're still a large part of what the book is about. Since then, we've seen the rise of the comedy drama. And I've written two comic novels.

I have attempted to both contract this new edition, removing whimsy, waffle and anecdote - and expand it, including more on writing funny across all formats. Radio, TV, novels, movies. Writing for one platform was never the best option, less so now.

Is it harder to become a full-time writer than four years ago? I think so. That's not what this edition of the book is about.

The emphasis is much more on becoming a better writer.

Writing funny not only because you'd like to do it for a living, but because you love everything about the process. If the profession ceased to exist tomorrow, you'd still get up every morning wanting to write it. I know I would.

You and I, we come from a long line of deluded idiots. We think we can change the world, make it a better place by introducing more laughter. We love the sound, warmth and healing nature of comedy and want to share it around.

I'll leave you as I did last time, with the oldest known Anglo-Saxon joke, from more than a thousand years ago:

"What hangs at a man's thigh and wants to poke the hole that it's often poked before? A key."

Somewhere on Twitter at this moment, someone is writing that line, convinced they're the first person ever to have thought of it.

Part One
In the Beginning

I want to be a comedy writer.

Now what?

This page has been intentionally left blank.

Apart from the above. And this. And-

1

Where Do You Get Your Ideas From?

You've watched the videos, attended the writing seminars, read the blogs and heard the advice. Don't worry about someone nicking your idea. Don't worry at this stage about getting an agent, yet. All you have to do to launch your comedy writing career is... make people laugh.

How? Hopefully this book offers a few pointers.

Where do you start? There are many approaches. Carla Lane, who wrote a ton of great sitcoms including Butterflies, The Liver Birds and Bread, apparently used to sit down and write. And write and write and write, until eventually her brilliant and hugely successful sitcoms took shape.

Anyone who has ever produced a finished piece of writing will admit there is an element of chaos around its creation. Father Ted scripts would feature half a dozen hilarious moments and the writers worked backwards to construct a script around them. Modern Family and Brooklyn 99 are quickly taken from the hands of the person who wrote the first draft, then pulled apart and stitched back together by a dozen or so of the funniest writers in the world.

What about us boring old mortals? It's good to start with a compelling character or pair of characters who want something they can't have – and usually their failure to get it is down to the flaws in their personalities.

We don't need to be talking just yet about sitcom scripts, finished novels or movies. It's enough at this point to imagine characters and set ups. The only gay in the village is a compelling character, and so is that horse who walks into a bar. Individuals who want something they can't have.

Writers think of ideas and in the excitement of the moment there's a rush to get everything written down, and to develop the concept.

"Where do you get your ideas from?" is one of the first questions writers are asked.

Despite the often sneering and stupid answers it receives, it's a very good one.

If you want to write comedy, or if you're already some way down the road to becoming a writer, you're going to need loads of them.

The correct answer to the question is "everywhere."

Let's take a step back and ask the even more obvious question:

What is an idea?

An idea can best be described in cartoon form, which is good news if you want to write comedy. It's that moment when our hero looks upwards, and a light bulb appears. It's a thought that lives independently of all other thoughts.

Your first job is to develop the mindset that makes you open to having these light bulb moments more frequently.

On its own it doesn't mean anything. You may be staying at a hotel where the manager, whose job is to be polite towards you, is rude and hostile. That's a funny idea for a comedy, you think. But that single idea will not survive in that form.

First, it needs to be hooked onto something familiar. For John Cleese, he recognised aspects of that character he'd been playing his whole life: mid-level authority figures who take charge not through any skills but a sense of entitlement. People whose default mode of conversation is sarcasm and whose response to being caught is to lie, lie and lie again.

Michael Palin plays an early version of Fawlty in the most famous of all the Python sketches. It's written by Cleese, who plays the customer who purchased a dead parrot.

An idea may arrive fully formed and ready to write, like the original pitch for Alien – "It's Jaws, set in space" – but most of the time we have to leave each one to stew. Meanwhile keep thinking of more ideas, one of which may eventually bolt onto the first and become a promising development.

How do you get your ideas?

When I say you get ideas from everywhere, I mean it's about approaching everything that you see and do with an open mind. Read, watch TV, remember conversations. Hold on to as much as you can, then write it down and see if it comes to anything.

Newspaper and magazine articles Did you know that Fast and Furious was based on a relatively obscure magazine article about illegal racers written in 1998? 642 movies later, that franchise just keeps rolling.

Short stories and novels Have a look at the TV schedules, check what's on in your local cinema. Probably around half of all the movies made are based on a book or short story. There's a reason TV companies keep returning to the same old classics, they're great stories that can be retold for each new generation.

To take a recent example, the highly original Wandavision grew from the back catalogue of Marvel comics. It was hugely inspired by The Truman Show, a film adapted from an episode of The Twilight Zone remakes, which in turn had been heavily influenced by the novel Brave New World by Aldous Huxley. Huxley said the idea came to him after reading Men Like Gods by HG Wells, and as "having a little fun at pulling his leg." Then he "got caught up in the excitement of his own ideas." Wells probably took his influences from Winston Churchill and the Bible, but I'll stop there for now.

A painting Did you know Wes Craven's movie Scream was inspired by, yes, The Scream by Edvard Munsch?

Conversation Before becoming famous as a novelist Chuck Paluhniak returned to his office job from a camping weekend where he'd been involved in a skirmish. His workmates were too polite or shy to ask him how he got his black eye. First rule of Fight Club...

A Building Of all the themes and ideas that appear in Remains of the Day by Kazuo Ishiguro, the one that sticks with me is the old stately home. Everything about that building is symbolic of the story. And lo it came to pass that Remains of the Day begat Gosforth Park by Julian Fellowes which lays this on with a trowel, and thus begat its TV follow-up, Downton Abbey.

There are so many places you can go for your ideas: Your memories, an interesting experience, a fascinating person you once knew, a lecture or class, holidays, a beautiful landscape. I'm sure you can think of more.

What do you do with your ideas?

Simple. Ask questions about them.

What if? What if the Scream painting came to life?

If only? If only animals could talk.

I wonder? What might the world be like if I give up and leave it now? For the answer to that, watch It's a Wonderful Life.

Wouldn't it be interesting if...? ...we could travel back in time and understand what the world was like in the past?

How do you recognise a good idea?

There are three simple tests that will help you decide if, at this very early stage, this is a good idea:

It grabs your interest Sometimes, you're walking down the street, minding your own business, and that idea you had yesterday pops back into your head. You start to see it playing out. Again, keep an open mind.

You tell other people, and it interests them You might be

surprised at how often new writers say to me "I've got a great idea but I'm not going to tell you it in case you steal it".

This is a common mistake new writers make: they might see a sitcom about a crappy Estate Agents in north London and shout "that's not fair! I had that idea years ago." Jamie Demetriou is a hugely talented writer-performer who created Stath Lets Flats. He had the same light bulb moment that you did but he was in the right place to turn it into a successful show.

I read hundreds of new sitcom scripts every year and in the last six months alone I saw three that were exact copies of pilots I've written over the years that have come to nothing. Don't worry, I won't be accusing you of stealing. Though I'll probably be annoyed if you get somewhere with your version.

<u>It's specific</u> We're still at the early stages, you've had a good idea, maybe you've taken some notes and started to get a sense of where it's going. You want to start imagining what it looks like, where it's set, what is familiar and what you are bringing that's different.

You may be looking again at your estate agent sitcom in which case, have you got something specific to say about it? Take a familiar idea and add a new detail. "You know 'Stath Let's Flats'? Well, this is a sitcom set in a similar estate agents, but the big difference is…"

What do you do with your good ideas?

The first thing you need to look for is **conflict**. I've read a lot of scripts that feature people arguing together in a room. This is not conflict, (yes it is Dave, no it isn't) it's people arguing. At the end of a conflict there are winners and losers. In comedy the losers have usually spent some part of the episode as winners.

Second you need to think about the **character** or characters who will best serve your idea. This is where things start to get difficult, and you have to be careful not to crowbar a person around an idea. Also be aware that if your individual has great promise, they might take you somewhere else, beyond your first idea. As always, but particularly at this stage of the process, be open to change.

Third, the more you interrogate your idea, the more **clarity** it will have. Sometimes you can get a long way with an idea. I have pages of notes about what I still think is a great idea for a sitcom. Hypocritically I'm not going to tell you it. But haven't yet been able to make it work. It needs more interrogation.

Based on a true story

This is something James and I often talk about in Sitcom Geeks, that the best sitcom ideas are the ones that you and you alone can write. That doesn't mean if something really unusual happened to you, that you have to stick to the whole story. Don't be afraid to fictionalise it. The actual truth is less important than the emotional truth you bring to an idea.

What happens when they don't work?

Don't expect your first idea to be your best. On the contrary, look at it as the first step to creating a much better idea.

If you can't get an idea to work – and don't be afraid to push it, hard – then drop it. For now.

Hang on to it.

Put it away, preferably in a place you can go back to the next time you're looking for ideas for new scripts to write.

Read a book. Watch a TV show. Look at a painting. Something new will turn up.

SUMMARY

Be curious about the world. Read more. Find things that interest you. Imagine taking the thoughts you have about stories or articles you read to unusual places.

Spend some time thinking about the concept. Are you getting excited by it? At this stage, you can do anything with it. Imagine you're in a maze. If you reach a dead end, re-trace your steps and try a new path.

Don't fall in love with the first idea. Be prepared to adapt or change it, or put it to one side.

Don't throw anything away. It may come in handy again when you least expect it.

2
The Blank Page

You're excited now. I'm hoping you didn't go with that first idea, but maybe you've chosen the second or third. You've spent some time thinking about it. Imagining the protagonists. Seeing them in stories.

You're worried that if you don't start writing this damn thing right this second, someone else will have the same idea and beat you to it.

The first piece of advice I would give is: don't write it.

Not this minute. And potentially, never.

One of the biggest myths in publishing is the Debut Novel. When a previously unheard-of novelist wins a big award there's a tendency to imagine that this must have been their first work. The Publishers play along because it's a much better story than the boring reality. The author's first book was okay, but the second was better and each time they improved. If you stop and think about it for a moment you can see the logic. When she won the Booker Prize in 2019, overnight sensation Bernardine Evaristo was a mere 25 years into her book writing career.

The same applies for sitcom. Peep Show was the first series Sam Bain and Jesse Armstrong made over which they had complete control. They'd written loads of episodes of shows before that though. Occasional exceptions prove the rule. Had there ever been a sitcom quite like The Young Ones? Never. It was the first and most influential alternative comedy when it came along. But it was also raw. Watch it now and you can see how so much that gang created that followed – Bottom, Blackadder, Ab Fab – was made of superior stuff.

You may be confident that your first big idea is brilliant but the reality is that so few scripts are made. Even if you're a successful writer who has had a successful sitcom on TV, that doesn't automatically mean another is about to follow.

Pete Sinclair, who writes sitcoms with Jack Dee and has for 40 years been about as successful a comedy writer as it's possible to be, had to wait six years before Bad Move, their follow-up to the successful and much praised Lead Balloon.

I know when I make these counter-intuitive statements that you may choose to ignore them. I know you are going to write it, despite all the odds against you, and anyway you think I'm joking, and I sort of am a little, but I'm also trying to make sure you understand that so little gets made nowadays.

If you're lucky, and it's brilliant, that script will at least bring you to the attention of producers and script editors who may be able to offer you work writing on other people's scripts. If you carry on producing great work, you may eventually reach a position where you pitch your own idea, and it may get made.

There isn't a right or wrong way to do it.

This is what I do before writing that script, screenplay or story. At the start of the process, day zero, I try and separate out a few questions to ask of my idea. It can – and should – take a long time to answer them. By the end I'll hopefully be ready to move on to the next phase.

It's almost impossible to answer one of these questions without referring to the others, but they break down into the following.

1. What's it about?

This is a nice simple question, and the hardest to answer. It should come in at around 25 words and be the boiled down essence of every answer that comes out of the next five questions. It's about a **person** (or two people) and **the world** they're in, the main **goal** and their primary **obstacle**.

If you take nothing else away from this book, be aware that

almost every piece of creative writing has these four essentials mapped out before a word is written. 25 words doesn't sound much but many hours of sweat, toil and staring into space are taken up by their creation. I shall keep coming back to this.

If it's about a bunch of flat-sharing 20somethings we need to know why this is not only not Friends, but it's something Friends-like with an extra ingredient no one has thought of before.

Don't worry if you haven't actually worked out what that additional element is, you're unlikely to find it until you start to investigate everything else.

Write your idea now. Go on. Have a go. It's going to change a lot as you go through the process of creating your work. Can you describe it yet?

2. What's it really about?

And this is where we find out it isn't any old 20something flat-share sitcom, it's Peep Show, which was one of the most original sitcoms of the last ten years or so. It took that old idea and gave it the big contemporary twist of being about the first generation to graduate from college with bleaker prospects than the one before them.

When we ask what is a show *really* about, we're looking for things that haven't been said before. This is the question to which there could be many answers. Fawlty Towers isn't only about a hotel owner in Torquay. It's what happens when you put a misanthropic character with a low opinion of humanity into a job that requires sensitive people handling.

And while Friends is about a bunch of friends hanging out, it's really about that crucial period in your life when you're still young enough to have crazy dreams about what you want to do, but old enough to understand that before long you'll have to decide whether to carry on living on the edge or settle for that cosy but dull mortgage-paying existence.

Often you can describe what a sitcom is *really* about using a well-known cliché to describe the story or one of the characters. Captain Mainwaring in Dad's Army, for instance, is "a little man against the world." Absolutely Fabulous is the female version of "the child is the father to the man." Many sitcoms including Frasier, Modern Family, Fleabag, The Simpsons follow the famous saying "you can choose your friends, but you can't choose your family." Many sitcoms, funny movies and novels are about a single character who is incapable of fitting into the world around them – "a fish out of water."

This is where you can go deep and philosophical. It's a serious business, making people laugh. You may think that there couldn't be two more different shows than Fleabag and Miranda. One investigates trauma, abuse, promiscuity and breakdown, the other features a large woman pratfalling in a fancy gift shop. Yet both are in their very different ways exploring the darkest, deepest questions about what it means to be a woman at the start of the 21st century.

3. Who is it about?

Every sitcom, comedy drama, screenplay, novel... every anything is about either one person wanting something seemingly impossible. Or a mismatched couple for whom the seemingly impossible is the idea that they can live together, happily ever after.

In the same way that your premise is taking something familiar and adding a new thing, there'll be features about your character we will recognize but with one new characteristic.

This is where the cliché describing what your show is really about is brought to life in an individual who may be "too big for their boots", a "loveable rogue" or "fish out of water."

Every character wants to achieve. "Next year we'll be millionaires" says Del Boy, "From now on I will make good every bad deed I ever did," Earl promises in My Name Is Earl. "I shall ensure that there'll be no riff-raff at this hotel," says

Basil Fawlty.

The above are all examples of external goals. They demand actions from the main character. This week's episode will revolve around our main person striving for this.

Lurking in the background, not visible to the human eye but working furiously - like the duck legs paddling under water to keep it gliding effortlessly across - is the internal goal.

Internal goals are so important. They are the unspoken desires, the urges we sometimes don't even know we have. The settling of scores, the arguments we have in our heads with people who don't even know there's an argument going on.

"I'll show my mother I'm capable of living my own life," says Miranda, "I'll show these idiots how smart I am," says Blackadder. Cher in Clueless, like Jane Austen's Emma, is so convinced she is a good person she can't see the harm of her actions.

Whether or not they succeed – or rather, because we are in the world of dreams and fantasy, *how* they succeed – is what your work is about. Apart from sitcom: what your sitcom is really about, if you're writing one, is how they *fail*.

4. Where in the world?

This is all about establishing a sense of place for your story. An anchor, which is a bold word to use with a straight face in a book about comedy writing.

It isn't necessarily where the main action takes place. Most of Friends happens in the two flats across the hall from each other, but Central Perk is often where each episode begins. And even though I'm not American, I understand Cheers partly because of the title, but also because the opening theme tells us it's the bar 'where everybody knows your name.' That's important because it's like "home" for some people.

5 Why am I writing this?

You may see people at work, or in your family, and spot something about them that's a glaring contradiction, but you haven't seen done in a sitcom or movie before. Tell me who the people are and the settings, and I could probably make a decent effort of creating it – but I probably wouldn't be able to add the personal detail and unique perspective you could bring.

By the way, this doesn't mean that because I used to be a journalist, I'm the best person to write a sitcom set in a newspaper office. Loads of comedy writers began their careers as journalists, and the first sitcom they write is set in a newspaper office (as was mine) and it never gets made (as mine didn't), so I'm saving you the bother.

It's less important that they were journalists, than that the bloke opposite you was a sexist bully or the prim woman in accounts was a secret stoner, or that when you went to the pub on Friday afternoon with your expenses tab, unusual things happened.

If you're going to mine your friends and relatives for comedy gold, be sensitive, creative and intelligent about it. Your interpretation of Grandma's screaming temper may be funny, but the rest of the family might not see it that way. And be careful not to libel people, unless you want to see the millions you make from your hit show handed over in legal costs.

But above all, this question is about you, and your emotional responses to the world you grew up in. It's about personal relationships, things that have happened to you, in a way that you are not necessarily repeating old stories, but making sense of the emotions you felt at certain times to do with those issues.

It's about bringing your singular emotional truth to a situation that resonates universally.

6. Why now?

Let's say, as we're talking about fantasy, you write a really brilliant script, and everyone loves it, and it gets sold and made. Even then you're looking at seeing it on the screen an absolute minimum of two years from now. Is it about TikTok video stars? The latest Tory Prime Minister? Or loom bands? In other words, will what you're writing now be out-of-date soon?

We'd all love to write screenplays that are timeless, but even the ones that stay with us for decades like When Harry Met Sally and This Is Spinal Tap caught the cultural moment of their era. It's impossible to predict what will happen in the next two minutes, let alone two years, but you should at least try to look beyond what's already out there, and speculate where we might be heading.

You might not even know you were writing about something, until years later the thing happens, and you discover you had predicted it. A review of Dad's Army written by Alan Coren in the 1970s described beautifully how the show worked because "behind the daftness lies a certain valuable poignancy which is not altogether explained by nostalgia. I suppose what I mean is they would have died too, if the greater folly had demanded it."

Dad's Army is every bit about the horrors of war as M*A*S*H. But how does that explain why the show continues to be successful almost half a century later, when nearly all of us Europeans have lived through an unprecedented era of peace, at least until 2022? I think it's pretty obvious, the show remains popular because it taps into our obsession with Europe – the idea that Britain once again finds itself standing alone against the rest of the continent. And you will enjoy that premise whether you are the most gung-ho Brexiter or the whiniest Remoaner.

That's a lot of questions to ask before you've written a word of your manuscript. It may seem an enormous effort, but it'll have you itching to get started and the more time you spend at this end of the process, the clearer your task will be as you carry on.

SUMMARY

In Chapter 1 you were thinking freely across an infinite canvas.

Now it's time to put some markers down. But there's still plenty of room and time to play around with your idea.

What's it about? Who's it about? Describe it using a cliché. Where is it set? Why are you writing it? Why now?

A character. The world. A goal. The obstacles. Have you got any of them yet? Try putting them together in 25 words. You may not get close. Don't worry, this is the first step of the journey.

3
Speak Up

"How do I become a successful writer?"

It's probably the first question you ask, and the response is always the second-least satisfactory answer you'll ever hear:

"You need to find your voice."

To which you reply, because it's the obvious follow-up,

"How do I find my voice?"

- and you're then told the least satisfactory answer you'll ever hear:

"We won't know until we hear it."

It's like when you ask: "How will I know if it's love?", and the indulging Smug Person in A Relationship answers "You just do!" Thanks. Really helpful.

We spend our lives trying to communicate our needs and desires as clearly as possible. It probably took you a few months from leaving the womb before you could utter a word. You'll have spent the next few years being taught to tell adults when you're hungry, bored, or soiled. The next few years will have been dominated by learning to live around strangers who happen to be the same age as you.

By your late teens or early 20s, you may have a reasonable idea of what you want to do with your life. If you want to be a writer, you've probably worked out there are thousands like you, but not so many actually doing it. That's when you begin the search for your unique way of expressing yourself.

Aware that "you just know" is not a helpful answer, here are some pointers: if I read your script and I want to carry on reading, because I genuinely have no idea what's going to happen next, and I can't wait to find out, then the chances are I'm reading a voice that's new to me. I will have laughed a few times as well, which you might not want to hear if you want to be the next Doris Lessing (one for the kids there).

Some more evidence you've found that voice: every character is distinctive. I immediately know who is talking, I can create pictures in my mind around what you've written. There's a point of view, although not something rammed down my throat. I don't necessarily like these people but from the beginning I'm curious to know more about them, you've hooked me with a story.

I want to know how it's going to end.

That's probably quite a helpful list to answer the first question, but I'm aware it doesn't go very far for the second. What Is Your Voice?

Your voice is the complete sum of you. Everything you are, every relationship you've had with friends, family and work colleagues. Everything you've done, read, watched. Everything you think.

Recall the experiences in your life – how you felt at key times, how you reacted to certain people at school, or in your family. How you learned to fit into your environment. Or more likely, since you want to be a writer, how you didn't fit in.

Which movie, piece of music or sitcom do you keep coming back to? Beyond its comforting familiarity, what draws you into the story, or the emotions?

When you're starting out, chances are your voice may be similar to one that's already out there, of someone or a piece of work you're obsessed with. For the first piece of writing you do, that's not necessarily a bad thing. Look on it as a way of showing you how to write, and getting the homage to someone else's idea out of the way early on.

Let me tell you about my first piece of attempted creative writing: a radio sitcom. I was in my early 20s, a journalist in a small town in South Wales, determined to move to London to make comedy. Sure of the destination, but utterly clueless about how to undertake the journey.

I wrote all six episodes, which as Simon Nelson of BBC Writersroom has pointed out is the very, very, *very* last thing you should do. Not only that, the piece was a crude rip off of three elements that were hugely influential on me at the time, clunked together unfunnily but which I was convinced would be snapped up by Radio 4 and broadcast within a few weeks.

I was already a big comedy fan, obsessed with the radio show Hitchhikers Guide to the Galaxy, the biggest inspiration for my masterpiece. Second were the novels of Kurt Vonnegut - coincidentally the inspiration for Hitchhikers itself. The third component of that script, the only thing that gave it a spark of originality, was that the protagonist was Jewish.

I typed the script with a carbon copy and posted it to the producer whose name I had heard at the end of each episode of Hitchhikers, Geoffrey Perkins. He agreed to meet me. I went to London and visited him in his office, where he admitted he had lost it. I dug out the carbon copy, which I sent to him. He lost that too. Nothing remains of my masterpiece. How brilliant was The Jewish Hitchhikers Guide to the Vonnegut? Luckily, the world will never know.

My obsession with Jewish humour was quite rare for an Englishman at the time. I'd read all the routines of and books about Lenny Bruce. One man represented everything I ever wanted to do in comedy, and only now I realise still does – Mel Brooks.

His great movie The Producers was such an enormous influence. It didn't just touch me as a work of comic genius – although I can only think of two or three other times in my life when I have clutched my sides in pain from laughing so much – it shaped my view of the world.

I was a teenager and didn't even know what "doing comedy" meant, but The Producers pointed me in the direction of the future I imagined for myself. That movie helped define my relationship with my family and the Jewish community I had grown up in, and was ready to leave. That sounds like a side effect but turned out to be a crucial part of discovering my voice.

Here's how Brooks describes his voice, during one of the many interviews he has done over the years for BBC2's Arena:

All my films are serious, you examine any one of them they're serious because they are passionate, and they depict human behaviour at given points in the history of humanity. You can't make a successful comedy that doesn't have any passion.

You gotta say something about the system, about the social structure, about prejudice, about people, about social behaviour. Comedy is not successful unless it deals with the system. The Marx Brothers, Laurel and Hardy – even Laurel and Hardy, you'd say, "well they're cheap comedies" – but they always dealt with the system.

He said that more than 25 years ago, and it still informs everything I try and do in my own creating. Writing this chapter has made me aware that my voice, whether I like it or not, is destined to continue as a less successful articulation of Mel's.

I've no idea how strongly Mel's words speak to you. You might disagree with everything, which is fine. But there's someone out there, a giant of entertainment who might articulate everything you want to say about the world. There's no shame in following the same route to humour as them. Make sure you bring your own views, neuroses and prejudices to the script.

Whatever you think of Mel Brooks, it would be hard to disagree with what he says about passion. That's become an over-used word in recent years. I interview people for courses who insist they are "passionate about comedy", which is as meaningless as adverts where oil companies tell you they're passionate about the environment.

Passions change over time but what I remember more than anything from when I was writing that sitcom was the passion. It was 1981, I knew that a new comedy world was opening up in London. I knew some of the people involved. But at that crucial moment I had chosen to leave them and follow my journalism career. Every planning meeting of Mid Glamorgan County Council I sat through, every petty shoplifting case I heard at Pontypridd Magistrates Court, every brass band concert and darts match and local amateur football derby I attended, reminded me I was a million miles from where I wanted to be.

I had no idea how to get there but was driven by the urge to escape. So much so that I could come home every day from a hard day's typing, sit at my own Remington and bang out hundreds of words of sub-Douglas Adams garbage.

Now that I think about it, this was a fourth element to my sprawling Hitchhikers Tribute Act that helped drive me out of journalism and into a comedy career. The urge to flee.

And we're back at the start, where trying to explain voice is almost indefinable. I would still struggle to tell you what my voice is today and am aware it's probably subtly different to what it was yesterday, or ten years ago. It changes all the time.

All I can say for certain is that in my early 20s, my comedy voice was not enough to get me work as a writer, but there was one element of it, yelling "Dave! You've got to get out of here! Writing this script is your only escape!" that set me on the path.

Getting the hell out of the life I was living was my "passion". What's yours?

SUMMARY

Who are you? What were the formative experiences that made you the person you are today?

How well do you know yourself? Be honest.

What are your obsessions?

Why do you want to write funny? What is driving you?

4
The Boss

Once upon a time, a long time ago, before Shakespeare, Plutarch and Jesus. Before Austen and Dickens and Trollope and Trollope, before even his Supreme Holiness of Narrative Elucidation Robert McKee, there was a book that taught people how to write stories.

It was called The Poetics and the author was Aristotle.

Student of Plato, teacher of Alexander the Great, astronomer, and according to Wikipedia "the father of western philosophy, the father of political science, the father of zoology, the father of embryology, the father of natural law and the father of meteorology." Not a bad list for the great Greek polymath known mostly to us as the Father of the "Writing Your Hit Screenplay" book genre. And no mention of the fact that he was probably the first receiver of a World's Greatest Dad mug.

For more than 2000 years The Poetics remained the only writing manual in the library. Consider this volume as homage, not the 983,473rd imitation.

The Poetics is short – so short, there appears to be quite a lot of it missing – but long enough to tell you Everything You Need to Know About Writing Comedy, Tragedy and Drama. Some say the lost parts dealt with further aspects of comedy, which sounds like the plot of the Hancock's Half Hour episode The Missing Page.

You can read it quickly and in full online, you'll find the short section on comedy included in the same part where he talks about tragedy.

That alone teaches an important first lesson about writing – tragedy and comedy have a lot in common.

"Comedy is tragedy that happens to other people" wrote the novelist Angela Carter. "I've always been drawn to that limbo of unease you get between comedy and tragedy," says Steve Coogan, uncharacteristically refusing to go for the perineum gag. Then there's that most famous quotation, attributed to 1950s American comic Steve Allen, that "Comedy equals tragedy plus time." Or, as the bloke down the pub would have put it straight after you'd told him your house had burned down: "One day you'll see the funny side."

Aristotle was the first to recognise that every story has a beginning, a middle and an end.

He defines it as the three-act tale: Act One is the beginning, the normal recognisable world at the start. Act Two switches the action, takes us into a different world where most of the story takes place; finally, in Act Three, the story is resolved. While there have been many variations on this formula, you'll find that almost every story you read, watch or listen to follows this simple structure faithfully.

Between each act there's a defining moment that twists the story round, and takes it to the next act and as Aristotle says, "complications ensue". Robert McKee calls these moments "the inciting incidents". McKee is a great communicator, and his books are literally and metaphorically the weightiest accounts, but even he acknowledges Aristotle said it all in 450 fewer pages, and for £25 less.

That basic Three Act structure can be applied to big fat novels, 90-minute movies, two-minute sketches and ten word jokes. In a movie, Act One is usually the opening ten minutes, then the twist into Act Two brings about an hour or so of complications ensuing, until the next big twist takes us to the end. Act Three lasts around 15 minutes.

Most movies are between 90 and 120 minutes. A joke, well written, can be told in a few seconds, but the same rules apply.

Short as it is, The Poetics isn't limited to the art of storytelling. The other area where Aristotle foretold the burgeoning industry of the self-help writing book was in his brief but accurate description of Character.

Each story, he explained, is the tale of a hero, someone we meet and recognise in Act One. That first inciting incident propels our hero in a new direction. The obstacles in Act Two are the twists and turns, the perils our protagonist faces, the epic trials and struggles that lead to Act Three. This is the final battle and inevitable, hard-earned victory. The hero triumphs, but that's not all. They have grown and learned, a different improved version of the person we met at the start of Act One.

It doesn't matter if you're writing comedy, tragedy, thriller or historical drama – Story and Character are at the heart of everything you do. And The Poetics answers every question you need to ask about structure.

There is one exception, in all those centuries and millennia of laughter and tears, one type that has failed to conform to the Aristotlean rule: the sitcom.

Sitcom characters never grow, and they never learn, and each episode is hardly ever a Three Act story. Act One and Act Two carry on along familiar lines: our (anti) heroes going about their lives when a crisis, or opportunity forces them to act. Act Two develops, the action escalates, and we approach that point near the end of Act Two where all seems lost – or won. The rest of the episode sees them not triumphing against adversity, but narrowly avoiding complete catastrophe. An episode of sitcom can often feel like it's stuck in a permanent Act Two loop.

No lessons learned, they come back next week, destined by the flaws in their character to make the same mistakes.

Sitcom characters don't go on a linear journey, they go round in circles and end up more or less where they started. Frasier will never be satisfied with his life, Edina will never grow up, Victor Meldrew will never come to terms with the modern world.

Isn't that also true of characters in tragedy? To some extent. They may die without having learned from their experience or heeded warnings, like Julius Caesar. Or they may have learned, but too late to save themselves, like Brutus.

In tragedy, characters die.

In sitcom characters live, but must return next week to die again and fail to understand why.

Which is actually quite tragic when you think about it.

In other words, I take it all back – Aristotle's decision to write about tragedy and comedy together proves he foresaw the creation of sitcom all along.

SUMMARY

Every story has a beginning, a middle and an end.

Even narrative sitcom, although that end takes us back to where we were at the start.

Characters go on a journey. In drama they learn something along the way.

In tragedy they learn, but too late, they die. Or they don't learn, they still die.

In comedy they may learn, and forget. But mostly they never learn.

Aristotle was a genius. You need never buy another screenplay book.

5
The Secret to Becoming a Great Comedy Writer

I'm going to step back for a moment and ask, why do you want to be a comedy writer?

Is it to begin a glamorous new life in showbiz (hollow laugh)? To escape the drudgery of a job you're not enjoying (drudgery, I'll show you drudgery)? Is it because you love comedy? Now we're getting somewhere. You'd love to be successful, but you'll settle for the pleasure of creating funny writing for its own sake?

Great. I can help you now. Wherever you are on the ladder to writing success, this piece of advice applies to all of you: the secret to becoming a great comedy writer is to become a great writer.

If your new year's resolution was to write a sitcom this year, my advice would be - wait three months. Learn how to write sketches. Wait another three months. Write more sketches.

If you want to be a novelist, you start by writing short stories. If you want to be a sitcom writer, you start by writing sketches. Forget your sitcom for now, and start there.

Sitcoms are the hardest scripts to get right. I gained additional insights into how hard in early 2022, after reading several hundred opening ten pages of your sitcoms.

There are nine skills you require in abundance if you want to be a great sitcom writer:

1. You need to be able to create compelling, flawed, funny, believable **characters.** Not just one, you need a minimum of two or three in every show, all interacting and making us laugh because of who they are.

2. Whether you're writing a comedy drama with a narrative arc or a self-contained sitcom where almost nothing changes, you need to be able to come up with loads of **stories.** They need

twists and turns, and all need to come as a direct consequence of bad decisions by your flawed characters.

3. You need to master the difficult art of writing **dialogue.** Conversations that sound realistic, and not something to be read by actors...

4. You need **jokes** ...and they need to be funny. Not only that, but the best jokes, like the stories, come out of the characters' flaws.

5. How good are you at **world creation**? Can you represent underlying themes? How easy is it for us to imagine the place you have created? I've read a lot of your scripts and I can see that it's hard.

6. **Structure.** A big thing happens early on. The main character responds, everything they do makes things worse; problems escalate until all is lost. How do they get out of it? I'm simplifying the process of creation but not much. Everything needs structure.

7. We can all get better at **self-editing.** We're too emotionally attached to our stuff. We miss gaping holes. Agonise over irrelevant changes. We all need to improve at this.

8. **Integrity.** It's okay, you don't need to display moral backbone in your writing, though that could be a plus. What I mean here is that the solution to the second twist in your story needs to have its roots in everything that has gone before. It has to be integral. All too often I'll see a twist which takes the scene or sketch into a new direction. Be faithful to what has been before.

9. **Self-awareness.** How honest are we about ourselves? The more we know who we are, the more depth of fallibility we can add to our scripts.

There's a simple exercise that you can do to get better at all of these and it's writing sketches.

I'm aware that nobody makes sketch shows anymore. Why should you bother?

Writing sketches is the limbering up exercise you need to do regularly to make you a better comedy writer.

In the 1970s The Two Ronnies was a training ground for John Sullivan and David Renwick. Years later Week Ending on Radio 4 was where sketch-writers honed their craft. Writers including Mark Burton (Madagascar, Wallace And Gromit), Simon Blackwell (Back, Breeders, Thick Of It), Georgia Pritchett (Succession, Shrink Next Door) and many more have gone on to write some of the greatest British audience sitcoms and TV shows.

Just because you can't find a home for them on TV and radio right now doesn't mean you shouldn't write them. On the contrary, there's never been a better time to create your own sketches.

If you can master the skills of sketch writing you can, very quickly, build up credits, and become known as a comedy writer that producers will want to employ. I'm making it sound easy, and of course the competition is enormous.

But as people move away from watching shows on their TVs, and attention spans continue to decline, the online two-minute movie is set to become one of the most efficient calling cards for a new comedy writer.

If you're still resistant to the idea of learning how to write sketches, here are some more comedy writers who began their careers creating them. French and Saunders made a number of sketch shows before Jennifer began to tackle sitcom in earnest - Ab Fab began as a French & Saunders sketch.

Simon Pegg and Richard Curtis started as sketch writers. Graham Linehan and Arthur Matthews were penning quickies for Alexei Sayle before they wrote Father Ted, and followed that with Big Train, possibly the most perfect TV sketch show ever.

If a sitcom is the equivalent of a one-act play, then the sketch is a short story.

These days it rarely lasts longer than two minutes, but in that time contains a tale that encompasses all nine skills mentioned above.

Some shows have recurring characters, but the truly memorable sketches are usually one-offs.

The beginning lasts a few seconds and establishes where we are and who is talking (5. World Creation). Then something happens: in comedy it's often called the "what if" moment (1. Character 2. Story).

What if the pet shop owner who sold you that parrot was like a dodgy car mechanic? What if the German soldiers suddenly realized they were the bad guys? What if the hardware store owner misheard every request you made for items and kept bringing you the wrong thing? There's your character, story and first big joke and we're only 20 seconds in.

More jokes now, we hope, as a consequence of that first big one (4. Jokes). Sketches are short and (3. Dialogue) must be snappy. You've got about a minute to escalate the action, to build to a second big moment (6. Structure). That incident must emerge from what's already been (8. Integrity) Then you've got almost no time at all to resolve that and get out of the sketch.

You won't get it right first time, but the more of these you write the better you'll become at (7. Self-editing), and the more of your own flaws and weaknesses you bring to the writing, the more likely you are to hit the funny spot. (9. Self-Awareness)

I've read thousands of sketches by writers at every level, and there is invariably one problem that stands out. Many people can write funny ideas, their "what if" moment can be hilarious, and the jokes that follow may all work, but it's that second twist that is nearly always missing from a sketch.

Many writers take the strongest joke from their middle section and try and pass that off as the punchline, but it's never a second twist.

What you're looking to do, just like if you were writing a full-length movie, is escalate the consequences of the twist at the end of act one, so three-quarters of the way through the sketch we've reached a point of no return, and a joke is required to twist the story out of act two and off to the end.

John Sullivan and David Renwick, amongst others, learned how to write long-running sitcoms having spent hours not just writing funny sketches but sweating over those endings. That's the kind of work you do where you don't always have quantity to show, but one quality ending to a sketch is worth the effort.

If you want to be good at sketch writing you have to work really hard at it, and it may take longer to come up with that second twist than the whole of the rest of the sketch.

A typical 30-minute sketch show will have 15-20 sketches, some very short and maybe one or two longer ones, but most coming in around that magic two-to-three minute figure.

That means hundreds of great ideas. It may look like you've got hours of material - but much of it won't work, and you want to know this script will deliver a rock-solid 30 minutes of funny sketches.

Sketches are incredibly hard work. Not harder than going down a coal mine, or teaching Spanish to 30 bored teenagers, but as hard as anything that can be in comedy writing.

Creating sketches online requires a whole range of additional skills that I won't go into here. But no amount of smart-phone savvy, editing skills or marketing genius can turn your two-minute movie into a viral hit across the world.

The most important point to remember is that every brilliant sketch, whether radio, TV or online, is already 95% great as a stand-alone piece of writing.

Give yourself a year to come up with a half-hour of sketches. That's barely more than one or two a month. Not much, is it? But you'll probably have to write five to come up with one good one.

You won't notice an immediate change. Your own life circumstances may be the same. But by the end of the year, I'm convinced you will be a much better writer.

SUMMARY

Don't go straight to writing your masterpiece. If you want to write a novel, start with short stories. If you want to write a sitcom or a movie, start with sketches.

Sketches are like two-minute movies. They comply to all the same rules of story, structure and character of longer form writing.

Start with "what if". Come up with loads of ideas. Characters, stories, goals obstacles. Just like those 25 words in Chapter 2, which we shall return to soon enough.

Part Two
An Introduction To Character

There are three types of comic tale. There's the Story of the Singular Man or Woman. Larger than life, the Monster, the Lone Battler.

Then there's the Story of the Mismatched Couple – two people brought together by life, or circumstances, or accident of birth, who somehow must find a way to get along.

There are Mismatched Couples in Monster stories: think of Gareth and Tim in The Office, Daphne and Niles in Frasier. But as the title tells us, the latter is all about one man. And there are Monster characters in Mismatched Couple stories, like Uncle Monty in Withnail and I. Again the title tells us that this is about a mismatched couple.

The third type of comedy is the Ensemble. TV producers have been looking for the next Friends since about Episode Three of Season One of Friends. Yet even Friends only became famous as an Ensemble during its success. It started as a vehicle for Courtney Cox and ended as the epic coming together of Mismatched Couple Ross and Rachel, who met in the opening three minutes of the first episode.

You may think you want to write an Ensemble, and I've read many scripts that attempt this.

Whatever you hope to write, whatever form, at the centre of every great work sits a person or group of people who can both be defined as, and in possession of...

Character.

6
The Monster You Know

In 2012 I was invited to attend a big BBC gathering in Manchester to discuss the future of TV comedy. Here I discovered from the then controller of BBC1 that what they were looking for, more than anything, was sitcoms "featuring monsters, and larger-than-life characters."

Instead of accepting this as factually correct and rushing home excitedly to create my new Godzilla-on-the-sofa masterpiece, I smiled indulgently, waiting for the conversation to move on. To provide some context, BBC1 had recently been enjoying the completely surprising success of two sitcoms that had initially slipped quietly into the schedules – Miranda, which began on BBC2, and Mrs Brown's Boys.

Forgive my cynicism. I've been to far too many of these gatherings over the last four decades to take it at face value, when a genuinely powerful executive has told a gathering of minions that The Thing They're Currently Looking For is a carbon copy of The Thing That Is Currently Successful.

Maybe there was a gathering I'd missed two years earlier where executives said, "We're looking for sitcoms featuring cross-dressing Irish comedians and larger-than-life posh English gals." In which case I take it back.

If we're to learn anything from this, it's that the best way for a show to become a hit is via word-of-mouth.

The controller had a point. If we look at our favourite narrative TV shows and movies, the vast majority have a single character at their heart. A monster, "larger-than-life", protagonist, antagonist, completely lacking in self-awareness, hideous, unlovable yet compelling misanthrope. Somebody who is always fighting battles without realising their biggest enemy is staring back at them in the mirror. Whatever we write, we are nearly always looking for that character.

If you know someone like that, and we all do, you should think about fictionalising them. Performers Steve Coogan, Jennifer Saunders, and Ricky Gervais all recognised individuals from their lives with those traits. Each possessed exactly the necessary amount of self-awareness to grasp that there were large elements of their own personalities in these people. Alan Partridge, Edina Monsoon and David Brent are exaggerated versions of Steve, Jennifer, and Ricky, placing their own worst faults under a microscope.

They are all writer-performers who remain at various levels in a position to develop their own projects. We ordinaries, and those for whom writing is the sole occupation, have to look harder and further, and do more work in the creation of our leviathans.

In the first episode of One Foot in The Grave, security guard Victor Meldrew is made redundant, and replaced by a machine.

Even before we get to know Victor, before Richard Wilson brings the character to life, before we become aware of the writer David Renwick's complete mastery of the farcical plot, we learn what the show is about. A man whose life has been defined by work, and not especially noble work, suddenly finds he's out of it. Too old to retrain, or learn new skills, he is now a man living at home with too much time on his hands.

David Renwick is one of the finest writers of our generation, One Foot in The Grave and Jonathan Creek two of the most sublimely perfect comic creations of recent times. We can only dream of writing a quarter as well as he does. It is possible to look at the simplicity at the heart of Victor's story to help us define our own monsters.

Victor's story is familiar, we've probably all known someone or someone's friend or relative who has lost their job while still young enough to find new work, but too old to be considered employable.

It may even be us. We may not be Steve, Jennifer, or Ricky but we know who we are, and while others see us differently, we probably have some pretty keen insights into our own weaknesses. Which doesn't necessarily mean your main character has to be a replica of you and your life. Separate that annoying trait about yourself from your personality, leave it for a while, then come back to it and give yourself permission to build a fictional character around it.

Recently someone pointed out that on Sitcom Geeks Podcast we tend to talk about the same characters over and over – the obvious ones from the hit shows. It's useful for us to do this, as most people will understand these reference points – but it's good to remind us that we tend to fall back on familiar names and faces, so I'd like to talk about two shows that rarely feature in this kind of pseudo-academic discourse: one by a writer and one by a writer-performer.

In the exact opposite way that Miranda being literally larger-than-life is an important aspect of her sitcom, Tom Hollander's size is an important feature of Rev, by James Wood (although Hollander is also credited in the early episodes).

The Reverend Adam Smallbone is a small, small-town vicar who has moved to a big church in a big city where he is supposed to be the cheerleader for the Biggest Story Ever Told. In Rev, everything else apart from the main character is larger-than-life.

The show deals with big themes like race, poverty, and the existence of God: here is a man looked upon by the community to provide all the answers but he's not even sure he's in the right job. All the time he is dwarfed by the huge problems of where he lives, the huge church he works in that echoes to the sound of emptiness and his own huge crisis of faith. Everything about Rev is about the exaggeration of size.

Monster is too harsh a word to describe Tracey Gordon, the creation of writer-performer Michaela Coel from the Channel 4 hit Chewing Gum. But the world and people she creates are big and broad. Tracey has one aim in life, to lose her virginity, and create the monster with two backs.

It's a familiar story, told in an original way. It's unusual for the lead in this kind of show to be a woman, and for such a well-drawn, flawed female character. The show has hopefully blown away the kind of fears well-meaning white liberal producers have had in the past about showing women and black people as weak, misanthropic comedy characters.

There are many larger-than-life aspects to this show. At one end of the spectrum sits Tracey's devoutly religious sister, almost as obsessed with sex as she is, and at the other her friends for whom sexual activity is part of their everyday life. In this sitcom the act of sex itself feels like the monster, our most basic human undertaking that we are expected to treat with religious respect and awe. Meanwhile all around us it's impossible to avoid its ubiquitous commodification, and assume that everyone else apart from us is doing it all the time.

As those two examples show, the word monster isn't confined to the characters. In John Carpenter's terrifically scary movie The Thing, the monster begins as a terrible beast but for the audience the most frightening monster is the fear that creeps up when none of the characters know who to trust anymore.

Your script may have one giant monster or several. At any given point in Modern Family, every one of the eleven or twelve characters in the ensemble is capable of acting like a monster. To return to that phrase larger-than-life, one of the most frequent problems I see in scripts is their closeness to real life. I'm not asking for cartoons and unbelievable stories, but it's always worth looking at your characters and seeing if you can't turn up the volume one or two notches.

If you decide that your sitcom is going to be about one person, they have to dominate. In their many different ways, David Brent, Lee in Not Going Out and Miranda dominate their shows. Every story involves them, every character exists in relation to them. Miranda's mum is arguably more of a monster than her offspring. There's room for more than one monster in your sitcom about a monster. As long as their monstrosity is feeding into the problems for your main character.

There can be few better sources of material for this than the monster you know, staring right back at you in the mirror.

SUMMARY

Stories can be about one character. In which case, they dominate whatever you're writing.

They may be monsters, or larger-than-life. Or in Rev's case, smaller. It's about how ill-fitting they are in the world you create.

A monster is usually a person but it can be your main character's psychological fear. It could be the obstacle.

Which reminds me, now would be a good time to revisit that 25 word logline. Has it changed much?

7

A Likely Story

In his entertaining memoir Conversations with My Agent, Cheers writer Rob Long talks about Bugs Bunny and Mickey Mouse, and how they relate to the world of comedy writing in the US. Every comedy writer, he says, wants to write Bugs Bunny. Nobody wants to write Mickey Mouse.

Mickey is cute (yuk) but Bugs is witty, Mickey is soppy (yuk), Bugs is mean and cruel and cool but don't we all love him?

I'd like to update this idea and talk about not just comedy writers, but performers, in fact the entire spectrum of comedy. This is the kind of massive generalisation that could get me a job as an online journalist, but I hereby declare that the entire comedy world divides into two: you are either John Lennon or Paul McCartney – yes, women and non-Liverpudlians too.

Lennon and McCartney represent a classic comedy set-up, the odd couple. Frankie Boyle and Michael McIntyre if you like. Now there's an odd couple sitcom I'd love to see.

In music and comedy terms, this idea of two giant egos in one band was exploited mercilessly in my second favourite film of all time after The Producers, This Is Spinal Tap.

The odd couple is one of the oldest comedy pairings in literature and theatre. Shakespeare's comedies have them, the 18th century duo of James Boswell and Doctor Johnson is a typical example, while Laurel and Hardy inspired several generations of physical and verbal comedy pairings.

Working on Horrible Histories I discovered that Gilgamesh, apparently the oldest story ever recorded, from thousands of years ago, has a mismatched couple at its centre.

In the comedy writing and stand-up worlds, everyone would like to think of themselves as Lennon. He was by all accounts a funny guy, and could easily have had an alternative career as a stand-up, or even a career as an alternative stand-up.

He was a fascinating complexity of contradictions: opinionated and generous, mouthy in public yet lyrically sparse, rude, and kind, an odd couple inside one person. Often downright unpleasant, a fighter who discovered pacifism, a misogynist who discovered feminism, a drunk, a druggie, a murderer (if you believe that bloke who specialises in writing memoirs that trash rock stars, explaining that he may have killed a sailor in Hamburg), taken before his time and a Working Class Hero. A British Bugs Bunny.

Paul – that's Sir Paul to you now, Sir Michael Mouse, darling of the establishment – is nice, and sweet, and just keeps making music, which is all he's ever done. He sings about frogs and raccoons and Mickey Mouse silly love songs, and the man's even got the nerve to still be alive. "Oh no" joked Mark Steel when George Harrison died, "The Beatles are dying in the wrong order." Lennon, like Bugs, remains loved by the rebels, while Paul has for most of his life been as enormously popular as Disney's number one iconic rodent.

The British comedy show that best illustrates the Lennon and McCartney love-hate relationship is The Likely Lads, featuring the characters of Bob, played by Rodney Bewes, and Terry (James Bolam). Written by the great writing double act of Clement and La Frenais, each character brilliantly represented an aspect of working-class life in the 1960s.

In the 60s there was just enough paid work, social mobility and house building for working class people to believe they could, if they worked hard enough for "the man", become middle class. Squeaky clean Bob wanted nothing more than to settle down in a nice little house with a nice little family, and that's exactly what happened. Terry was angry, he wanted more, he was inquisitive about the world, and for his troubles, ended up joining the army.

In the 70s when they were successfully revisited in Whatever Happened to The Likely Lads, the differences between Bob and

Terry were as heightened as they had become by now between John and Paul. Terry lacked the millions of John, the New York arthouse lifestyle or the exotic conceptual artist wife, but for both him and Bob the 60s dream was over.

The differences were more marked and the comedy harsher, but the odd couple at the heart of that show were totally believable. And as Bob's dream of suburban bliss crumbled before him, the standard message of the British sitcoms of the time remained intact – whatever type of working-class person you might be, remember your place and don't try to rise too far above it.

The Gilmore Girls comedy drama is one of the greatest odd couple shows. At different times mother-daughter Lorelei and Rory are Abbott and Costello, Patsy and Edina, Groucho and Chico, Thelma and Louise. Lorelei and her mother also have a great Bette Davis-Joan Crawford thing going, while Rory and her friend Paris are frequently as funny a pairing as Jerry Seinfeld and George Costanza.

Occasionally I like to look at some of the relationships I have with comedy partners. I work with other writers, producers, performers, and directors. What are the extremes of these couples? That's where you'll find good comedy because it's based on the truth of your own personality, but an exaggerated version of it.

In some cases, I feel very much like Lennon, the naughty boy in the class who will say something to get a reaction. In other relationships I find myself reining in the other person, trying to bring our extreme comic ideas back to some kind of centre ground, hearing a little voice sneering "crowd-pleaser" into my ear.

I could squeeze this Lennon-McCartney analogy dry but the point I'm making, hopefully, is that mismatched couples produce great comedy.

By the way, Paul never used to get any credit for his love of obscure conceptual art (he introduced John to Yoko), his amazingly innovative work as a producer and his continued ability more than half a century on to stay in tune with the best contemporary music. John's been dead over 40 years, but it took Peter Jackson's extraordinary Beatles documentary Get Back to do full justice to Paul's story. And to show us how even in the shadow of Bugs Bunny, Mickey Mouse is compellingly flawed and worthy of exploration.

SUMMARY

The best couples in comedy are usually mismatched. Opposites attract. Which doesn't mean they have to get on.

It's one of the oldest and most enduring ways of creating comedy: putting two people together in a room and forcing them to get along.

Look at your own life. Examine aspects of relationships where you can highlight the differences between yourself and the other person. There's comedy in there if you dare to look.

8

Show Some Character

I'm aware that I'm contributing more than my fair share to a growing genre of what may loosely be called "tips about writing." The way things are heading this type of book will be overtaking crime and YA fiction by next Wednesday. I'm also aware this is time I could arguably be spending better, writing my own shows and pitching new ideas.

And I'm further aware you may wonder why you should be taking advice from someone who is writing about writing, while a host of his peers are far too busy writing comedy to write about writing comedy.

I write about writing partly for selfish reasons: I genuinely believe my comedy writing has improved since I began teaching 16 years ago, and that I've had more writing work since I started to write and teach about how to get more writing work. Which still isn't much use to you. But I'm also interested in the process, and what other writers have to say about it.

Recently I read the latest collection of writing tips in a national newspaper from famous novelists, because like you I want to know. There wasn't a great deal of original insight, but among the usual platitudes I've read a million times – "try and write at the same time every day," obviously given by someone who's never had to work in the vicinity of small children, "write every day" yeah yeah very original – there was one that stood out.

"Ignore tips," was the headline for advice given by one novelist. My instinctive response was, yes I've been there too, that's exactly the kind of counter-intuitive comment I like to say, to remind people that rules are there to be broken. But then it continued, specifically naming "character, setting, description, plot" as unworthy of meriting any advice at all. And this from someone who teaches a creative writing course.

If I can offer one piece of advice that works not just with writing, but everything in our lives: if someone says something that you disagree with profoundly and on every level, don't immediately mock them.

Stop for a moment and ask yourself why they said it. Do they really believe what they're saying? Are they deliberately trying to annoy you? Does it deserve a response?

I read his piece again, and decided that, on reflection, weighing up all the arguments advanced, he was talking total bollocks. As I might say at some point in this book, "Always trust your instincts." What he did make me realise, though, is that we often repeat standard phrases without thinking. "Comedy is all about character" is one of those phrases you hear all the time, but it's hard to find anyone genuinely explaining what they mean by that.

It's bugging me because I read a lot of scripts, from writers at all levels of experience, and at some stage I'll notice inconsistencies in how characters are portrayed. I notice it watching comedy on TV, at the movies and in novels. It's quite rare to see brilliantly crafted individuals and I think it's because we don't pay enough attention to who our creations are at the planning stage of writing.

I looked up "character" in the dictionary, and the main definition, which suits us well, is "the aggregate of features and traits that form the individual nature of some person." Yet we use the word loosely, and with contradictory meanings.

Sometimes we say that a person has character, meaning they are good to be around in a crisis. But we also say a person is "a character", meaning they're colourful, or you have to be careful in their presence. The opposite, in fact, of someone you'd want to be around in a crisis. Jake Peralta in Brooklyn 99 manages to be both.

In general, when creating a new story, the starting point will be a person, the protagonist. Audiences want stories about people being challenged in their lives, and to see how they overcome those challenges.

That's why novelists and screenplay writers put so much research into their creation. Only when those writers know everything about the person are they able to put them into the story to see how they respond. Each individual will be pushed to their limits, and must find something from within themselves to overcome their difficulties.

This is where "showing character" applies most specifically in books and movies. In comedy, as with drama, the redemption that arrives around the last third of the story invariably comes from the weakness we have been highlighting in the previous two.

In sitcom nobody ever triumphs. Characters fail without knowing why, the following week they come back and fail again.

Which is possibly why we comedy writers are maybe less thorough as we bring to life new creations. Isn't it enough to say that Monica is a control freak? Or that Larry David has no social filter? As long as we can keep coming up with funny stories that expose their comedy flaws in the harshest light possible, do we need anything else?

There are a few issues I keep seeing when I watch comedy on TV. A character has a funny scene but there's another person with them and, although this character should also be funny, or even just interesting in the scene, they're often only there to give the funny person someone to talk to. Or I'll be reading a scene where two or three people are all saying funny stuff, but the jokes are interchangeable, and I forget who the individuals are.

New drama shows and big-run children's sitcoms on TV often draw up a "Bible" – this is a document that lists all the characters, their back stories, families, everything we need to know about their worlds. American cartoon series occasionally have them, but it's rare to want that much detail when you're coming up with a movie or a six-part comedy show. When Steve Coogan creates a new character, one of the first things he wants to know is "what car does he drive?" We can see how relevant this is for Steve Coogan, as it would be unnecessary for the rest of us.

For the great writing partnership of Marks and Gran, whose shows are often commissioned in bunches of 13, I can see how a bible may be useful. Richard Curtis never has one. Take your pick.

I do think we aren't working hard enough to flesh out our comedy characters, and over the next few chapters I'll be looking at how we can show some.

SUMMARY

Character is defined as "the aggregate of features and traits that form the individual nature of some person."

Writers don't always work hard enough to develop their characters.

In comedy, we're less interested in the backstory detail, more about the flaw in their personality that makes them act in a funny way.

9
Getting into Scrapes

As I was working on an idea for a new sitcom character recently, I heard myself asking this question of her – why is she always getting into scrapes?

It's a phrase that will be familiar to anyone over 50, the kind of thing that used to be written about characters like William from the Richmal Crompton Just William books. "Whether he's dodging his rotten sister Ethel or getting into scrapes with his band of outlaws, there's never a dull moment with William Brown around."

William belongs to a forgotten era of cheeky chappies covered in mud, with grazed knees and short trousers, and predates the teenager, glue sniffing, video games, Mr Beast or whatever it is that da kidz are running with today.

Despite that, it feels like the perfect question to ask of a comedy character. It works quite well for secondary characters in novels and screenplays, and even for the main characters, though they may change and become something different. It feels particularly applicable to sitcom. I'm not sure why, but once I asked the question, I found it was simple to answer for every successful sitcom character I could think of.

Not only that, but the answer also told the story of almost every episode that character appeared in. Once I started to think about how these answers worked for my new character, it quickly brought to life something that until then had seemed abstract.

The clichés that we sometimes use to describe characters in sitcom are signposts to how they will get into scrapes. We often talk about people who "say the unsayable", and this characteristic is key to almost every Larry David plot in Curb Your Enthusiasm, the basis of Alan Partridge in his many manifestations, and David Brent.

Have we seen enough of this character for now? Possibly. I often see him in new scripts (invariably a he, though not always) and have yet to see anything that moves us on from the "LADs" – Larry, Alan and David. When you're creating a new character, if you're going to take something that's already out there you need to give it a fresh twist.

A great example of this was Phil Dunphy from Modern Family. For decades we have been enjoying characters who get into scrapes because they are trying to be something they aren't – the "square peg in a round hole".

Captain Mainwaring and Gordon Brittas are leaders without authority; Hyacinth Bucket and Citizen Khan the square pegs trying to fit into the round hole of what they believe to be a higher social status; Basil Fawlty and Bernard Black of Black Books perfectly unsuited to the jobs they choose to do. Reggie Perrin was always trying, and failing, to be an individual in a corporation where survival required conforming with the crowd.

In Modern Family, Phil got into scrapes trying to be the dad his dad was to him. This was exactly the opposite of what he needed to be – but always, by the end of each episode, he found happiness when he stopped trying too hard. A sitcom character who learns from his mistakes? Yes, but only for a moment. He was back the following week, making the same mistake.

However many times we admit we're wrong, for the sake of family unity or the chance of a quiet life, we'll continue to make the same mistakes. That's a great example of taking a familiar human trait and giving it a modern, believable twist.

The William Wordsworth line "Child is father of the man" seems to resonate with comedy writers, and there are many adults in sitcom whose childlike behaviour gets them into scrapes. Dougal in Father Ted and Kramer from Seinfeld are two great examples who provide their writers with a constant supply of marvellous bonkers stories. Edina Monsoon in Ab Fab approached middle age remaining steadfastly teenage.

One of the reasons we see so many characters based on these old sayings is that they offer a wealth of comedic possibilities. Jake Peralta in Brooklyn 99 is a beat cop whose childish behaviour often gets him into trouble, but is also at the heart of what makes this such a charming show. He manages, as discussed earlier, to both "be a character" and "show character" when in a tough spot.

Characters who are "mad as hell and not gonna take it anymore!" as Peter Finch yelled in the movie Network, will inevitably head for scrape-land at high speed. The only question you ask when watching Victor Meldrew is not "Will he lose it?" but "When?" Rik in The Young Ones is in a state of permanent excitement, and George Costanza's anger, which we become aware has been inherited from the previous generation, sits in stark comedic contrast to Jerry Seinfeld's equanimity.

George is a beautifully complex original, he also gets into scrapes because he tries to be something he isn't. Like Lee in the first eight series of Not Going Out, he wants something he can't have – "You can't always get what you want," sang Mick Jagger. And George has poor communication skills, a guaranteed scrape enabler for Moss in IT crowd and almost everyone in Big Bang Theory.

"Say what you mean and mean what you say" is a helpful piece of advice, and there are many characters whose inability to do that can cause problems. In Yes Minister and Yes Prime Minister, civil servant Sir Humphrey never says what he means, which makes it pretty hard for the already indecisive Jim Hacker to mean what he says. In Ever Decreasing Circles, Ann Bryce is trapped in an unhappy marriage and forced to lie continually, because she's scared of the consequences of admitting the truth.

There are many examples of characters "sticking it to the man", but rarely with great success. In Porridge, Fletch's little victories allow him to survive, but only to spend another day in prison. Hawkeye in M*A*S*H is "his own man", but only in the context of working every day stitching up wounded soldiers from the frontline of a war he hates. And as for Rev's ongoing battles against the biggest boss of them all, there can only be one winner.

This isn't an exhaustive list, or a scientific one. Think of a cliché like one of the above that might describe a place you are at, or may have been in your life. If it reminds you of how everything you tried had the opposite effect of what you were hoping to achieve, you might find it takes you to a world of comedy and misunderstanding that you can exploit successfully. You don't believe it? Next year you'll be a millionaire.

SUMMARY

What makes your lead protagonist get into trouble?

Is there a phrase or a cliché you can use to show why?

Think of your favourite characters from comedy you love. What is it about them that gets them into scrapes?

10

I'm Not Who I Think I Am

"There's two sides to every story" is one of those great clichés of writing that deserves more serious examination.

I'm sure it applies across all genres, but I only know about comedy, where so much of what we write hinges on the difference between how a character sees themself, and how the audience see them. BBC Comedy Head Jon Plowman called it The Gap. Not the shop, but the space between those two places, where comedy resides.

All of us have a number of character traits and these are usually covered by a broad spectrum, but "two sides" is a simple shorthand way of getting us to pronounce those qualities in a more extreme form.

In a movie, or a novel, there is time to explore the spectrum, and the complexity of who personalities are and why they behave in a certain way. In sitcom you have less than half an hour, more like 22 minutes if you're working for anyone apart from the BBC, to tell a complex and satisfying story about your main character or characters.

Whatever you're creating, the quicker you can arrive at the funniest part of what sits at the heart of your lead player the better.

When you're creating a new person, a good place to start is your copy of Roget's Thesaurus. Buy the book, cheapskate, it's so much more satisfying than the online version, and it helps broaden your vocabulary in the process, although proceed with caution with regard to verbosity, loquaciousness and, like, using too many word thingies where you can get away with not using too many word thingies.

If you have a rough idea about the kind of creature you want them to be, it will be helpful to look up a key word you might use to describe them and see where this takes you.

For this experiment, I've looked up the word "rigorous". It comes in a block of words headed by "accurate", and includes the definitions "precise, exact, detailed, meticulous, scrupulous" and even "perfect". Nothing too bad yet about this person, wouldn't you say?

However, included in that same small block of definitions are the following words: "pedantic, hair splitting, nit-picking."

Already you can start to create a picture of this new character. They see themselves as thorough individuals with a sharp eye for detail and an ability to arrive at the correct answer. You and I see them as the kind of irritating, controlling perfectionists who make our lives a misery, when they're not annoying the hell out of us.

It's fun to look at some of our favourite comedy characters and find two words that describe them which essentially mean the same thing but offer a positive and negative side. If Jez from Peep Show was asked to describe himself in one word, he might well come up with "spontaneous". And that's not a bad word to describe him, suggesting excitement, curiosity, and a willingness to take the initiative.

Ask Mark to describe Jez in a word though, and he would probably call his flat-mate "impulsive". It's a similar word, but is probably far more accurate, and gives us more insight into the brilliant stories that follow in each episode, suggesting reckless, selfish, thoughtless, rash, foolish, hair-brained... okay I'll put the thesaurus down now.

In real life most people are not so extreme, but this is not real life, it's fiction. All that's required is an element of believability, and familiarity. We've all known someone like that in our lives.

If you want to see the extremes of personality in action, look no further than the on-going story of our daily news. Politicians and sports performers offer perfect examples of characters who have two very strong characteristics. At different points in their careers, the thing that's perceived as their weakness will become their strength, and vice versa.

My football team Leeds United have for most of my adult life been the most despised in the universe. In 2019 their great new manager led them back into the Premier League by creating an entertaining side that won over the grudging respect of even their most hated adversaries. By early 2022 the exciting adventurous attacking style that Marco Bielsa had imbued in the team had been rumbled by almost everyone, and they let in more goals in a month than the eventual Champions did for the entire season. Bielsa's great strength was also his downfall.

Way back in 2018, in a British galaxy long ago and far away, when the first edition of this book came out, I wrote about a British Prime Minister called Theresa May. Remember her? The one before the one before the one before the current one (for now).

In April 2017 she was enormously popular, so popular that she felt emboldened to call a General Election. In these volatile times, she said, what people wanted to see more than anything was strength and stability. Mrs May possessed huge amounts of both of these marvellous characteristics. Right up to the point that she didn't.

Within days the story had changed. Theresa May was weak and unstable. Look, everyone! See how she twitches when she's asked a difficult question! Look at all the times she shakes her head before she answers! Watch the strong and stable backdrop literally come crashing down behind her.

She became the permanently damaged leader of a permanently damaged party. (Imagine, a Prime Minister losing the confidence of their entire front bench?) Every new test proof that she was utterly useless. Still in charge of the country, just. Still turning up for work every day. Getting up in the morning, looking in the mirror, saying "I'm still in charge." At which point the mirror wobbled and fell off the cupboard, narrowly avoiding slicing off her big toe.

Off to the market to buy a pound of apples. The shopkeeper charges her £10, she tries to haggle and ends up paying £11.50. See how it's possible for a person to think they're one thing, for the rest of us to see that they're exactly the opposite – and for both groups to be right.

It was like Yes Prime Minister, except every time that phrase was uttered it was done with deep sarcasm. Thank goodness that could never happen again.

SUMMARY

Who does our character think they are? Who do we think they are? The gap between them is where the comedy lives.

Think of a trait for your character. Look it up in your thesaurus. The bigger your thesaurus the greater the choice. Find two meanings that give different impressions of that word.

As a rule, it's probably not a good idea these days to refer to someone in a book as "the current British Prime Minister."

11
Off Up D'bugs Losa!

Are comedy writers putting in enough work when creating new characters? All too often you see people in sitcom, stories and movies responding to situations in random fashion.

Novelists and screenwriters spend an inordinate amount of time building character profiles. I don't believe sitcom writers need to think as much about backstory or what our comic inventions eat for breakfast.

We sometimes over-think these definitions. I occasionally read character descriptions that appear to have been created out of random word selections from that Roget's Thesaurus. "Mary is bubbly, vivacious, almost irritatingly so but she can be a control freak at work and mean to her mother... Jim is outspoken yet tactful, rigorous but slapdash, generous but thrifty."

Whatever you're writing, movie or sitcom, comedy or drama, there are several strong traits that the best characters possess.

Ever fond of the naff acronym, I've bundled these numerous features into the just about readable but utterly meaningless OFF UP D'BUGS, LOSA. I'm sure there are more letters to add, and these aren't necessarily correct, but here goes:

Before anything else, your new character must be that – new. **Original.** It's okay for them to be recognisable, it helps the audience because they don't need so many signposts to guide them to the jokes, but they need something else. Mrs Brown may be identical to Mrs Boswell in Bread, but the canny meshing of old school stereotypes (she's a man in drag) and post-modern tropes (let's break the fourth wall and have Mrs Brown acknowledge, Garry Shandling-like, that the audience is also in the room), somehow equals hit TV show.

I doubt if the first person who springs to mind after you mention "Hugh Grant" is "Tony Parsons", but the latter's first novel Man and Boy is remarkably close in structure, character and entire story to Four Weddings And A Funeral. The first-person character in the novel is more nuanced than Grant's, it is a novel after all. But the book is effectively a working- and middle-class version of Curtis's super toffs movie. And don't sneer, it's a gently amusing and surprisingly moving read. Parsons' creation then was totally original, and yet, in a seemingly contradictory phrase, he is also **Familiar.**

Here are some more examples of individuals who managed to be familiar but original. In the 80s and 90s, several extremely different chaps emerged who were nevertheless pretty much the same guy. This was the geezer defined by what many people of my age say either with dewy-eyed nostalgia or hate-flecked spittle – Thatcher's Britain. He was emboldened by the view that if you want to get on in the world it's okay to cut corners, cheat the taxman, trample over the person in front of you to get what you want.

The most obvious embodiments of this were Del Boy from Only Fools and Horses, and Arthur Daley in Minder. But there were others. He may have been living in previous centuries, but Blackadder of series Two, Three and Four was the Del Boy of his day. A chancer who saw a gap in the market and understood straight away how he could fill it. Father Ted may have trained to devote himself to the care of others, but on Craggy Island there was only one person he was looking out for and that was Father Ted.

They must be **Flawed.** This is possibly the most complicated part of characterisation. It's easy enough to say this is a person quick to anger, and has been given a job in customer services. But you need to find a way to sustain that premise, otherwise the character just gets sacked, end of story.

I'm remembering a person I once saw getting on the bus, a tightly clenched ball of simmering rage. I looked closer and saw he was carrying a book about Buddhism. Maybe he knew he had anger issues and was finding a way to deal with them. In comedic terms I would write that as someone who sees himself as a calm, karmic, cosmic Buddhist, who comes across to us as a tightly clenched ball of simmering rage.

They should be **Unsatisfied.** This will be the source of many of your stories. Sometimes you'll have a protagonist that things happen to, but it's always a stronger call to make them drive the story. Which leads to the next part of the acronym.

I wouldn't so much call this a characteristic, but it's very important for your leads to be **Proactive.** I read a lot of scripts from writers of all levels, and find whole scenes go by in which our hero passes the time of day, and nothing happens. They may be engaged in amusing banter, but it's largely inconsequential.

For the next letter I thank our finest comedy script editor Andrew Ellard. Andrew writes wisely about **Difference**, which he explains is what most comedy is about. How do your characters react to the same piece of information? The answer is a great way to help define who they are, while ensuring that every character in your script is there for a reason.

If you're consistently finding it hard to differentiate one character from another, you may need to ditch one of them completely. Better to do that at this stage than when you're struggling to get through your first draft.

Your character has to be **Believable**. To make what may seem like a fine distinction, "believable" is not the same as "real". Real people, in general, are dull. Even if we live exciting lives, it's quite rare for us to become embroiled in some ridiculous situation, largely of our own making. That we proceed to make worse by our actions. And lead us to some epic situation that will probably be resolved during the course of New Year's Eve in Trafalgar Square, or however British movies end these days.

I doubt if any of you have ever seen someone get out of their broken-down car and smack it across the bonnet with a snapped-off tree branch. But we've all experienced that feeling of rage and frustration, and understood the urge that drove Basil Fawlty to his act of arboreal violence.

A trait that applies specifically to sitcom is that people never learn from their mistakes. They are **Unteachable.** Will Basil, having got into such terrible trouble by lying and lying and being caught out as a bald-faced liar, start telling the truth? Or next time will he try and be a little more devious? You know the answer and admit it, you do it too, give that failed strategy one last go. You never learn do you? Still working on that comedy screenplay aren't you? (Spoiler alert: it won't get made, but if it's great and packed with superb characters it might get you work as a writer for hire.)

This next one is so important I could devote an entire chapter to it. For now, have a look at this, and come back to it later.

Every hero, anti-hero, protagonist, antagonist, lead person in everything you'll ever write, must have **Goals.**

There are two types of goal – external and internal. An external goal is specific. It's out there. Might even have a time frame. "Next year we'll be millionaires!" That sentence informs every dodgy caper in every episode of Only Fools and Horses. Niles wants Daphne. Jake Peralta wants to solve the crime.

You want to be even more specific. Give your character a thing to desire. And because this is comedy, they almost certainly won't get it. But let us enjoy the subtext of every line, every action, betraying their desire to the audience.

External is always out there, in plain sight of the audience. But what about the internal goal? This is some emotional requirement that stems from their upbringing and environment. We don't need to know the backstory. We can tell this person wants respect, or to be listened to, or to show that annoying relative that they can amount to something.

And because this is comedy, they almost certainly won't get it.

Your character has to be **Sympathetic.** This, by the way, does not mean likeable. Reggie Perrin's boss CJ is an insufferable pompous bore with a mean streak, but he's the boss, and we all understand that he didn't get to where he is today by being likeable. (Also, I recently had a light bulb moment in which I realised that The Office is The Fall And Rise Of Reginald Perrin, with Tim as Reggie and Brent as CJ).

Finally, the word often associated with British sitcom characters – loser. Written here it's LOSA, which stands for **Lack of Self-Awareness.** Returning to The Office, there is the clear moment at the end of the Christmas special where for the first time ever, we see Brent understand how utterly despised he is. Within a few minutes the entire sitcom is finished, forever, the end, at least until the comeback tour a decade later.

Some of these traits conflict with each other. Characters, like you and I in real life, can be contradictory, but the more we can define their funny ways, the greater their contribution to your story.

SUMMARY

The most original creations are usually familiar, but there will be one new aspect about them. You don't have to stray too far from what's already out there to build your new monster.

Use the above chapter as a check list to ensure that you gain maximum comedy from your protagonists.

You may not be able to come up with versions of all those characteristics. But there are four that you can't do without:

- Familiar.

- One original trait.

- Proactive.

- And have goals.

That's your minimum requirement.

12

Knowing Me Knowing You

Congratulations! You've created your first great character. They are flawed. Have goals that they'll never achieve precisely because of those flaws. Are proactive in seeking those goals, which makes them the architects of their demise.

Now all you need to do is create another character, yes? And another? Build your stories around them.

Almost every piece of writing advice about creating character is focused on the individual. This is the most important part of that "who's it about?" question we asked at the start of the book. But no one, including me in the first edition of this book, has spent enough time on an issue of equal concern.

People exist and thrive in comedy only in relation to those around them.

A troupe of beautifully defined individuals in your script will only come to life when their conflicting goals and selves crash into each other like fairground dodgems.

It's not the most crucial character trait for Basil Fawlty to say "he is in a loveless marriage." Yet it's impossible to look at his schemes and lies without thinking about Sybil. The show Miranda stars Miranda as Miranda but so much of the key to her comic personality is clarified during the infrequent but memorable scenes with Patricia Hodge as her mother Penny.

Even where the other characters exist almost completely in relation to the larger-than-life monster - think Gareth, Dawn and Tim in The Office – those supporting roles are vital in building a picture in the audience's minds of Brent.

We've spent some time looking at mismatched couples, and where the sitcom has this as a central premise, it's clear the relationship is one of the major aspects of the show. At this early stage in the invention of your new creation, while you're still working out who they are, it's worth taking time to think about the key connections between your leading characters.

One approach is to imagine the "sit" for the characters in your "com".

The parent-child relationship is probably the most frequently explored narrative across all forms of storytelling, from Oedipus Rex to Star Wars, calling at Hamlet, Lear and all strops between.

Miranda and Penny is straightforward enough, they are mother and daughter. But your story can have a parent-child relationship at its heart without having to be about parents and children. Del Boy and Rodney are siblings, as the series develops and characterisation becomes more important than story, Del becomes the father-figure and Rodney eventually escapes from his shadow.

You don't need the two of them to be related. Dougal is a child-like figure in every situation, but Ted is also a father figure - with a small 'f' in this instance - if not a reliable one. Fletcher and Godber in Porridge, Blackadder and Baldrick: both of these relationships have strong father-son elements.

Why is this such a common relationship story in drama and comedy? Principally because every child's relationship with their parents is both unique to them and universal. Each one of us knows about the parent-child relationship, even as we experience it in a different way to one another.

The frequently quoted opening sentence of Tolstoy's Anna Karenina encapsulates this: "Happy families are all alike; every unhappy family is unhappy in its own way." You may not have had an unhappy family life but there may still be unresolved issues. Things you always wanted to say to your parents, now it may be too late.

Returning to the "why me" question, only you had the experience of growing up as you in relation to your parents. Or whoever brought you up. Often some of the greatest storytellers discovered that elusive "voice" because of the absence of a father or mother figure.

If you want to start building connections between your evolving characters, it won't do you any harm to give some thought to the strongest connections you've ever had, which began the day you were born.

The second most common link with universal resonance is the sibling relationship.

Not everyone experienced this, but for those who did there are bound to be individual slights and scars that could last a lifetime.

Until recently sitcoms about siblings were rarely sighted. The two most familiar shows from the 20th century were Friends and, in the UK, Sykes – starring Hattie Jacques and Eric Sykes. In both cases the sibling relationship played a minor part in the comedy. (In case you were wondering what a show called 'Friends' might be about.)

The big change came with Modern Family – and even then it took a while to get going. In episode seven of the first season Mitchell and Claire bond as they remember their teenage figure-skating days. From that moment the sibling relationship becomes central in many of the episodes.

Since then, we've seen excellent sibling comedy in series such as This Is Us, Fleabag and Grace and Frankie. Your show doesn't need to be about siblings but think about the dynamics. Older brothers and sisters believe they carry the burden of responsibility. Younger ones resent the authority their elders carry from having enjoyed those early years as the only child. It's quite possible to see that kind of relationship play out between a couple, or two friends.

Speaking of friends, or rather, Friends. The most popular sitcom in the history of the universe still casts a long shadow over every new show that seeks to put a gang of 20something mates together in a room, or New York coffee shop.

Friends are trickier relationships to develop in comedy writing. Families can and do fall out frequently, but they're stuck with each other. Friends fall out and drift away, make new friends. Or become more than friends. You can see how the iconic eponymous series started to creak under the weight of struggling to keep Rachel, Monica and co together as their relationships began to resemble a hostage situation.

Sitcom characters are in it for the long haul, they need to fall out but you don't want it to be so bad that they stop seeing each other, because that signals the end of your show's life. As my co-host James Cary says whenever he reads a scene with a friend being horrible to their mate, "Don't stand for that. Just leave!"

How about enemies? That feels like a more promising and less frequently excavated comedy mine. Work would be the obvious place for this, both characters trapped because a job is a job, even if you hate it.

Gareth and Tim had some of this going on in The Office but that was several plotlines down the order. There's an ideological chasm between Leslie Knope and Ron Swanson in Parks and Rec, but a grudging respect that keeps their feuds at a manageable level.

My favourite enemies were Jerry Seinfeld and Newman. Even now I can't look at those words without spitting "Noo-man!" in Jerry's angry sneer. Like all the best enmities it appears to have emerged from some incredibly minor spat. Something about the post in the lobby. It spiralled into a completely irrational animosity, not sustainable for more than a couple of minutes in occasional episodes, but a believable relationship.

There are many other connections you might choose to look at. Neighbours. Teacher and student. Boss and employee. Everyone has stories to tell, think about yours. They are both unique and universal. Start researching them now.

SUMMARY

Even while you're developing your characters, you should be thinking about them in relation to each other.

Examine your relationships with the adults who brought you up.

There will be aspects that are unique to you.

Examine all the relationships you have with friends, relatives, figures of authority. The postman in your street. The shopkeeper you see every day. Who are they? And who are you?

13

The Family Family

Outnumbered by Guy Jenkin and Andy Hamilton is a show I have enjoyed immensely over recent years. It allowed people to use the words "BBC family sitcom" without offending the gods of cool TV. With Modern Family in the US and Here We Go on BBC1, new life has been breathed into a genre that felt like it hadn't moved on since the 1970s template Butterflies by Carla Lane.

Indeed, the phrase "family sitcom" was often used as shorthand to describe everything that was wrong with British comedy. And it's easy to see why. My Family was a big hit with audiences for its first few series, but as programmes like Peep Show and The Office came to prominence, people found it harder to accept the artificial nature of the audience sitcom. The presence of small children added to the sense that the show was mawkish.

I worked on My Family for a series, and although it dealt with a number of hard and tricky subjects, nobody could see past the cosy faux artisan kitchen and comfy living room furniture.

Inspired directly by shows like My Family, Guy and Andy – two of the most experienced and brilliant comedy writers in the country – went in the opposite direction and created a model that combined a non-audience realistic feeling with the best aspects of the audience family sitcom.

Outnumbered takes the classic family sitcom set-up – mum, dad, stroppy teenager, bonkers pre-teen and cute youngest - and removes the studio audience. In the early days when the kids were younger they slightly improvised the script. This meant the kids didn't sound like they were spouting words from a page, but instead were talking like real people.

If you're hoping for a career as a comedy writer you should study Guy and Andy's record. Like many of the best writers already mentioned they began by sending in sketches to topical radio shows. That was nearly 50 years ago. Since then, together and apart they've written on and created some brilliant comedy shows, including Drop the Dead Donkey, The Kit Curran Radio Show and the movie What We Did on Our Holiday. For every show written they have had a dozen turned down, as they told us in Episode 150 of Sitcom Geeks.

Like many top comedy writers, they have remained largely unknown outside of the business. If you know Andy at all it's probably through his acerbic contributions to News Quiz and Have I Got News for You, or the great radio series Old Harry's Game, in which he plays The Devil.

You'd think no one would ever want to make a family sitcom again in the old style. But the TV networks can't get enough of them. Sitcoms are nearly always about putting people together in a room who would rather be with anyone else, anywhere else.

"Family sitcom" is such an all-encompassing phrase, especially if you consider that programmes as diverse as Steptoe and Son, The Royle Family, Fleabag and Fawlty Towers can be included.

You can look at many other s and think of them as part of the family family. Porridge is an obvious example, substituting the metaphorical prison of family life for a real one. And it's not stretching the analogy too far to cast Mackay and Barrowclough as the harsh husband and his well-meaning wife, with Fletcher protecting Godber like an older brother shielding his innocent sibling.

Writers are always looking for short-cuts to create their stories. I'm aware that this book is attempting to distil my 40 years of learning, failing and occasionally succeeding into separate compartments that you can refer to as you put together your work.

Occasionally a writer spots a pattern that is worth investigating as a potential way to build your story.

Arrested Development writer Mitch Hurwitz has identified four types within family that are visible in "every" sitcom. I'm not sure I would go that far but there is some merit to his definition of 'Matriarch, Patriarch, Craftsman and Clown.'

The Simpsons is one of the clearest examples of this: matriarch Marge, patriarch Homer, craftsman Lisa and Bart the clown. They aren't necessarily gendered as written. For example, in the sitcom of the same name Hurwitz refers to Roseanne as the patriarch, Dan as the mother figure.

If you're struggling to make your stories work, imagine your characters not necessarily as workmates, or friends sharing a flat, but as siblings, or mother and son, or husband and wife. Wasn't The Office one big unhappy family? Daddy Brent stomping around all over the place, mummy Tim clearing up after him?

Or with Seinfeld, you can imagine Jerry as the dad, a typical American sitcom dad. He puts food on the table but is otherwise a loving observer of his family's foibles. George is the neurotic mum (who tries everything and fails) while wacky son Kramer is always getting into scrapes and daughter Elaine keeps falling for the wrong guys.

There's a whole range of American sitcoms that you wouldn't think of as family, but which conform to many of the genre's forms. The great M*A*S*H, like Porridge, has a group of people forced together who end up acting like classic sitcom family characters to maintain their sanity. This was followed by Cheers and Friends, which offered a refuge from the traditional idea of what a family is, by creating families of their own. Cheers and Central Perk were both Home.

Recently, when I've been trying to develop new sitcoms, I've started to imagine, for the purposes of character and story development, that every sitcom is a family sitcom. It's a great way of helping to define your stories, as well as giving your characters reasons to push against each other.

It works whether you're writing a sitcom, screenplay or novel. If you're wading through a scene, struggling to bring it to life, imagine the characters as members of the same family: sisters, parent-child, first cousins. Not for the sake of it, for most of us family relationships are the first and deepest relationships we know. In many ways we're attracted to new friends when there is something familiar, or familial, about them.

Imagine a scene or chapter you're writing about a boss and their immediate subordinate. Are they in a parent-child relationship? Or are they like a husband and wife? Are the people close to them closer to one or the other of the main characters? Is one of them always trying to prove themselves to the other? However you answer those questions will help give some direction to your story.

I can't imagine I've heard the last BBC bod on a panel tell an audience they're looking for sitcoms featuring "the monster". Instead of tutting and sighing at this complete abdication of originality – I do that too, but try not to dwell – why not accept this requirement and attempt something different within it? Maybe look at that monster as a spoilt child?

That immediately gives you two secondary characters, one who indulges it and the other who tries to fight it. Already you've got something that might potentially be interesting, without having to resort to the clichés of family sitcom.

SUMMARY

The family set-up remains one of the most popular and enduring structures for comic narrative.

Even if you're not planning to write about a family, you should borrow the dynamics of family relationships for your characters.

Some of the most successful TV sitcoms use the family structure in a non-family setting – Cheers, Friends, Seinfeld.

Think about your own family experiences and relationships. Be aware of what's driving the tensions between people.

14

My Favourite Characters Are Lumps of Wood

There's a star in every audience sitcom that rarely gets a mention, yet has the potential to be one of the most useful members of your cast. Every show has them, but most writers don't bother to give them the attention they deserve and require. I'm referring to: the room.

It's not any old room, it's your "sit". That's already half of what you're trying to write, so you should give it a good deal of thought.

In the opening minutes of the pilot episode of Frasier, the writers introduce us to Frasier's stunning, arty, European-style flat. Martin, his working-class retired cop dad, comes round for the first time and is unimpressed. "Nothing matches" is all he can say. "It's eclectic!" is Frasier's defensive response.

Within a few minutes, not only are all the characters perfectly established, but we find out that Martin will be moving in with Frasier. And with no prior warning, Frasier has to watch, horrified, as Martin's hideous easy chair is wheeled into the centre of the room. "It's eclectic!" he tells his furious son.

And there the chair stays, for the next 200 or so episodes, a visual representation of so much of the comedy of that show. An inconvenient and garish carbuncle plonked in the middle of Frasier's perfect world, the physical representation of Martin. He doesn't even have to be in the room. That chair is a constant reminder of Frasier's seemingly ideal life, forever intruded on by his father.

It's a wonderful example of how you can add layers of meaning to your script without having to write more words. And it's a great way for drawing you back to the sitcom every week.

One of the things you're always trying to do as a writer is create a universe that audiences want to keep returning to. Hogwarts. Punxsutawney. Frasier's flat. There's something comforting and grand about the place, it's always interesting to look at. But that bloody chair is always centre stage, a funny reminder of how Frasier and his dad are always close, always clashing.

The same applies to screenplays. Much of the genius when it comes to memorable sets is down to the set designer, working on the stage in the days before the shoot with the director and producers to create something that looks exactly right for the movie.

You can help them. I remember reading a sitcom script by the writer Adam Lavis set in the world of entertainment TV production. Using a few words to describe the desks of the male and female producer he brilliantly and hilariously created a world, while setting up two of the lead characters without them even being in the room.

The woman producer's desk was tidy and efficient, all colour coded folders and neat piles of scripts. The man's desk was a file-free zone, but was covered in wacky toys and gadgets. I worked for many years on Channel 4's Big Breakfast show, and there was a constant battle between clever, funny and brilliant women trying to get a show made and male producers who worshipped the laddish Chris Evans and Jonny Vaughan. The men arsed around with the toys on their desks, while taking credit for any success regardless of their contribution.

If you're not already famous in another field of writing, the first screenplay you sell is unlikely to be greenlit with a multi-million-dollar budget. This makes it worth your while to think hard about where most of the action takes place, and how you can use that to comic or dramatic effect.

The great movie Clerks was famously made on a budget of $3 or thereabouts, and was filmed entirely in downtime at Kevin Smith's local store.

We tend not to think too much about the "sit" because it doesn't seem as important as characters or plots or jokes. But it can help you establish some of those characters and jokes, as well as the world you want people to come back to.

This is especially true with audience sitcoms, which are limited to two or three main sets. That's what your audience sees week in, week out.

Jerry Seinfeld's flat is another great example of a room that is part of the show. There's nothing unusual about it, but it's the place where everything begins and ends – the comedy stage. Jerry is the host, "master of his domain", the MC of the room, and each of the three regulars is given a large free space to shine, gesticulate and stomp around.

By complete contrast, in the other main set of the show, the cafe, everyone is cramped round a tiny table. This is where the rudeness is often at its funniest, when the four of them are literally within spitting distance of each other.

The café in Seinfeld seemed like a familiar and universal representation of the typical greasy spoon diner. The notion of what was meant by café as social space was about to be transformed by Friends. That show established the coffee shop as a happening place for young pretty people to meet. When I was their age you went to a café for nothing more romantic than a fry up. You certainly didn't go to hang out, or heaven forbid, drink their disgusting coffee.

Without Friends, the Starbucks culture may never have happened. I'm not asking whether that's a good thing, merely pointing out the enormous impact of Central Perk, and how that "sit" added one more layer of meaning to one of the most successful sitcoms ever.

When I'm watching a British audience sitcom my attention sometimes wanders, but even if that had happened during an episode of Frasier (it rarely did), my eyes would have been drawn to something relevant to what I was watching – a stunning work of art, a beautiful table, oh, Martin's hideous chair.

In British sitcoms the distraction might get me annoyed. Why is that living room the same as every living room I've looked at in every audience sitcom since 1973? What is this room telling me about the people who inhabit it? Nothing, that's what. But I could still describe to you the Steptoe household, what an amazing set, a surreal yet totally believable representation of what an old rag-and-bone man's house may have looked like. They frequently spent entire episodes in that one room.

Why does your protagonist act in a certain way? Is there too much clutter in her life, so she misses something important? You can show that in a room. A big pile of unopened mail in a corner would do it: occasionally looked at, then run away from.

Is everything in place, perfectly, too perfectly? Is this person a control freak? Again, as the attention of the audience wanders it can suddenly be brought back into focus by a tiny movement from our main character, to correct something that looks slightly out of place, but only to them.

Next time you watch a movie, look at the work that goes into the rooms that are used regularly. If it's a British movie, I bet you can come up with half a dozen ways of improving it.

SUMMARY

Character, story, jokes. Your number one priority. But give plenty of thought to your setting.

You can describe a character by the setting. One cleverly defined object can bring your characterisation to life.

Coffee shops. Living rooms. Bars. The venues are the same. Think about the elements in your story that will make them distinctive.

Part Three
An Introduction To Story

Character is story. Story is character. Is it really that simple? Well yes, when put like that. All you need to do is come up with characters and stories that are both familiar and original. That's the tricky bit.

There's another tricky bit, which is the way we use the word "story", which causes endless confusion and irritation. Particularly to me. This is the molehill on which I won't die but will stub my toe and angrily shout at the sky.

When I talk about story, I mean "this week's episode." When other people talk about story, sometimes they mean "this week's episode". Other times they mean "premise". Theme. Underlying Truth. Robert McKee's book is called Story and it weighs a ton so you can bet your life it's not about to tell you how to write The One About Your Lead Character's Birthday.

This week's story is not your Premise, or Theme or Underlying Truth. It is a self-contained tale that doesn't carry through into the next episode.

That doesn't mean it exists in a different universe. Usually, the way your character drives that story – episode! - involves the underlying theme. In a novel, it's one of the many side plots that are contributing to your main premise.

In this week's episode, Jake Peralta will try and solve a bank robbery from 20 years ago. That's the story. But in the process, he's hoping to impress Santiago's father. Jake's always looking for a father figure, that's part of the premise.

"Confused? You won't be," as they used to say at the start of Soap, the superbly nonsensical 1980s American sitcom.

If you are still baffled, don't worry. It's time to separate out the strands of character and story.

At least for this episode.

15
Plot Plot Plot

Character character character. I know, I keep going on about this. When we're creating our new piece of work, we tend to separate out plot and character as the two big areas to concentrate on. Which makes life simpler when you're staring at a blank screen.

However, everything is connected, isn't it? That's something I've learned writing for Horrible Histories. That show sees the world not as I learned History at school, as a neatly compartmentalised sequence of events, but a messy realistic ongoing catalogue of the story of all humanity.

Henry the Eighth had six wives, Alexander the Great and Genghis Khan crossed the globe and vanquished huge swathes of it. Boudicca almost singlehandedly chased the Romans out of Britain. All stories come back to the same recurring themes of character – the lure of power, the things we do for love, the feeling of never quite being satisfied with what you have achieved. All these stories happen because of those people, and the strengths and flaws at their heart.

In his essential guide Writing That Sitcom, James Cary presents a thorough and perfectly detailed system for creating stories that can work for whatever you're writing. His method is to generate dozens of one-line ideas, without thinking too much at this stage which might work best. Get the concepts out there, worry about fleshing them out only when you have so many that you're spoilt for choice. This is not a bad place to start, and it works for James.

My approach is slightly different. I find it almost impossible to think of stories for a new show or book without imagining how the characters will respond to them.

To take as an example the kind of banal plot they would never have used, what if a character on Peep Show won the lottery?

No character on Peep Show would ever do the lottery, is your correct answer. Hear me out. If Jez won, he would spunk it all on a party that would go horribly wrong. If Mark won, he'd keep it from Jez, but Jez would find out and make him spunk it all on a party that would go horribly wrong. The second is most like a Peep Show story, then again the first would be like Peep Show taking the piss out of the naff plot idea that "Jez wins the lottery." He would win, throw all the money away on a crap party, and we'd move on. Plot taken care of in two minutes.

At this early stage of developing a script, I find thinking about how the story might advance will help define my currently half-formed character. If the story starts to feel wrong for that person, there's still a chance that it's something wrong with the character. If not, then it's a plot to put to one side, and maybe test against another person later on.

Once you have a great list of ideas to choose from, and decide to go with a particular story, there are a number of aspects to develop. To show that I don't spend all my spare time thinking up acronyms, I've chosen here only things that begin with "P".

Starting with the obvious, but then the obvious often gets ignored because it's too obvious.

Plan: The more work you put into the detail now, the more you'll get out of it later. A typical main story in a typical sitcom has anything between six and ten "beats". A beat is a moment that advances your story, "I won the lottery!" That's a beat. "I went to work and told the boss to stick my job up his arse!" That's another.

Your character wants something. You're going to keep putting obstacles in their way, they're going to have to overcome each one. Each move will take your character deeper into their crisis, or opportunity. Eventually you're going to have to bring them back from the brink. This is one of the hardest parts of writing, you're not just testing your character, you're testing your own ability to invent new ways of telling stories that test them. And keep audiences guessing what will happen.

Personal: If you can get something from your own life that's great. When he was a jobbing writer, Larry David famously argued with the boss on Saturday Night Live and quit on the Friday... then had second thoughts on the weekend and turned up for work the next Monday, pretending the row hadn't happened. This became the basis of a great Seinfeld episode for George. Your life is the starting point. Sitcom plots are not like real life but if there is a basis in your unique perspective, you can bring something fresh and original to a story.

Proactive: This was a "P" I discussed under character: to give your story more energy it will help if your lead character desperately wants to do this – or stop it happening, and they will do whatever they can to achieve it.

Knowing that this is your flawed comedy character at work, the bigger the investment at this stage of the story, the bigger the problems when it all starts to go wrong. And we like big. Big is good. Big is where laughs happen. Not the story driving them. It's so easy for a character to become passive. And that's one P we must avoid. Make your characters make things worse.

Point of no return: Three quarters of the way through – all is lost (or won). I read a lot of scripts and get three-quarters of the way through only to find the story meandering gently to a predictable ending.

British sitcoms are usually made in blocks of six a year: if you're lucky enough to get six scripts commissioned, is it that difficult to imagine six times a year where you nearly got something and failed, or nearly lost everything and just held on? Maybe your character is about to get together with the partner of their dreams. Or lose £10,000 and get beaten up, or arrested, or sent to prison. It literally cannot get any worse – or better. And you have a quarter of the show left (six or seven BBC minutes, four or five anyone else), to arrive back to where your heroine was at the start of the episode. Nothing has changed, nothing has been learned. You have to find a way out of it.

Pendulum: We tend to think of plots as a series of escalations that take us deeper into the situation until we reach that point of no return. But wait – the thing your character always wanted has suddenly appeared, and instead of being in a terrible place, they've succeeded. Of course, this success will be fleeting, but it will help make the fall that follows harder and, hopefully, funnier.

The pendulum is especially important if your sitcom is principally about an odd couple. How often in Modern Family does Cameron's perceived success spell disaster for Mitchell? Only for the situation to have swapped in the other direction within a few moments. That's classy, extremely well-planned plotting.

Peril: You can't have a point of no return if there's no peril. The deeper the character gets into trouble, the more likely they are to be in peril. I'll be honest, peril is almost the same as point of no return, but it helps to emphasise how big a deal your point of no return must be. And impress you with the number of P's I have.

Pathos: Not every sitcom has or needs pathos. "No hugs, no message", Larry David (again) famously said about Seinfeld. Yet for me one of the most enduring features of that sitcom is the relationship between George and Jerry. Jerry has lots of success with work and women and a full head of hair. George, even when he starts to become successful on all but the head-of-hair fronts, cannot enjoy the success. He will always sabotage good things. We know people like this, sometimes we are that person, it can make us sad even as we're laughing.

Pathos happens because characters in sitcom never learn from their mistakes. We don't have to like them to sympathise when they fail to learn.

Punchline: There's nothing more satisfying than a big funny character-driven joke to round off an already hilarious episode. Like when Basil drops the vase when he has been accused of stealing money to bet on a horse. Moss working in the bar at the gay play in IT Crowd. George, having pretended to be a Marine

Biologist, describing how he saved a giant whale from sure death. I remembered those episodes probably because it's so rare to see such a satisfactory ending. In all cases you had shows, writers and performers at the top of their game. You may not be at that place yet, but you need to try.

And finally...

Persist: Those complicated character-driven plots don't write themselves. Providing your characters are right, and your story has developed how it feels it should, not how you were hoping to make it work to suit your needs, then you'll get there in the end. Most of the time, we settle for an ending that isn't quite r.

SUMMARY

The more work you put into plotting your episode the better. Plan in as much detail as you can.

All the above suggestions are important when formulating your plot.

But two of them are essential.

First, your protagonist must be proactive. This is a mess of their own making. A direct result of their personality flaw.

And second, there has to be a point of no return. We'll talk more about the all-is-lost moment later, but everything you ever write needs this to happen around three quarters of the way through.

16
Why Are We So Rubbish at Plotting?

When I started writing narrative comedy around 30 years ago there was nothing like the Landfill of Writerly Wisdom currently available, to which I have become a regular contributor.

Around that time, I wrote five screenplays. Not one made it beyond first draft and few to final draft, let alone Final Draft, if that even existed then. This was the 1990s and one of the few books that offered writing advice was The Foundations of Screenwriting by Syd Field.

Syd's formula was relatively simple, so simple that I could hear a voice mocking me every time I followed it. It's a long time since I owned a copy but from what I remember his approach to screenwriting was mathematical.

A screenplay runs between 90 and 120 pages. Anything less is too short, anything more is too long. A big thing has to happen on page 17. Not 16 or 18, that shows you don't have a clue what you're doing. If your lead isn't fully immersed in their final great quest by page 84 then your script is in big trouble.

I hadn't thought about that book for ages, his screenplay-by-numbers style had long been out of fashion. Recently it has returned to the fold, courtesy of Blake Snyder, whose Save The Cat screenplay writing guide is one of the better additions to the aforementioned Landfill.

After reading dozens of your scripts in recent months I took away two big notes. The first was that we don't work hard enough on our initial ideas.

The second was that plots were not working.

I wondered if it was a more fundamental problem at the heart of storytelling. How often do you walk out of the cinema swept away by the twists and turns of the story, satisfied as the final credits roll that you have witnessed a magical journey from start to finish?

I recently finished a book by a well-known novelist, a few years ago it was shortlisted for prizes. It's funny, a bit dark, has patches of brilliance. The writer is great on so many levels. But the story was all over the place.

I find this problem everywhere, people ignoring probably the oldest and soundest piece of writing advice ever, from Aristotle about 2500 years ago, which essentially breaks down to "every story has a beginning, a middle and an end." Why is this so difficult? I don't know.

Maybe the answer is mathematical. Perhaps Syd was onto something after all.

Let's revisit our schooldays. Imagine for a moment that your script is represented by a line on a graph. Along the bottom axis we have time. The period that elapses during your work.

Your manuscript can be anything – sitcoms usually take place over two or three days. Dramas and movies can cover weeks or months and novels can take place over several years.

Up the vertical axis we record tension. You might want to use a word like stakes. Crisis. Opportunity. Whatever you choose, it's something that needs to increase as you work through the crucial points in your script.

Step 1 – 0-15%

According to Syd, having set up your characters and established your world, you want your big moment to happen around 15% of the way through. That means, sitcom writers, that you have little more than three or four minutes to introduce your characters, create your world and present your lead character with a big crisis or opportunity. Which we shall call Step 2.

Step 2 – 15-15.001%

This step is getting its own little stair, even though it lasts for barely more than a few seconds. Robert McKee calls it the inciting incident. It's going to turn your story around.

What this is not: This is not the Theme, the Premise, the Underlying Truth, the whole reason you want to write it, the leitmotif. This is the moment an opportunity or crisis arises for your main character...

Step 3 – 15.001-30%

...how they respond as your character is more about the theme. Right now, let's see what happens to this specific story. It has involved a complication and made things worse for your main character. I don't want to take Syd too literally, but maybe I should, and if you're writing a sitcom another three to four minutes feels like a good amount of time for this next moment in your story to play out. 10 to 15 minutes in your movie.

Step 4 – 30-45%

The consequence of that complication of the initial consequence has combined to make things even more difficult. If you're writing a much longer piece, you need more complications and consequences, so in your movie or novel I would expect to see steps 4 a), b) and c) happening here. And careful not to make it a cyclical chain of problems and solutions. Every solution must become an escalation of the problem.

Step 5 – 45-60%

If you're writing a sitcom script for anyone other than the BBC you're now around halfway through your story and an advert break is about to happen. But even if not, you want the end of this step to be a moment that leaves vital questions hanging. So vital your audience will want to come back from their toilet break to find out what is going to happen next.

In his essential book Into the Woods John Yorke talks about the midpoint. We tend to overlook this because we're always structuring our work around big end-of-act moments. The midpoint can best be described as the moment of realisation. It's when Johnny Nash sings that he Can See Clearly Now. He can see all obstacles in his way. What is he going to do about them?

Step 6 – 60-75%

That question you left hanging in the air was a big one for your main character. As big as anything they've had to deal with in their lives. And, as we're heading to a critical point-of-no-return, the next response will have the biggest consequences of all. Everything is lost – or won.

All this time, I hope, the line across your graph has been moving upwards. Not steadily, because each step is caused by a jolt that was a consequence of the previous one. Which doesn't mean you're suddenly throwing a plot from nowhere at your main character. These stories are escalating because of the behaviour of your main character. Your characters are, in a phrase I use frequently, the architects of their own demise.

What happens now? How does your character escape? In drama, novel and movie land, they will find some inner resource that we realise was there all the time. They'll use that to power their way through to the end of the story, where they will emerge having grown and learned.

In sitcom terms, your character will somehow extricate themselves from this torrid pickle, but only so far as to get them back to the place they started. No growing or learning for them.

How do we engineer this without the audience noticing? If you don't know the answer, all will be revealed.
Not yet. You'll have to wait until Chapter 33 for that. Meanwhile, stay tuned...

SUMMARY

Plotting is all about structure.

There are a few key points that every story must have:

- an incident near the start that sends your heroine off on her journey

- a place somewhere in the middle where she can see what's required to make it to the end

- a moment, around three quarters of the way through, where all is lost

- an incident that twists the story again and sends said heroine to the end of the journey.

Unless she's in a sitcom, in which case she's heading back to where she started, none the wiser.

17
Can You Make a Drama Out Of A Comedy?

Everything we've talked about so far has been in relation to a self-contained episode. The structures dealt with can be used for sitcom, movie screenplays and novels, but have mostly been explored in relation to the big difference between comedy and all other forms of storytelling.

Everybody and his dog these days is asking you to write comedy drama. TV commissioners want them. Publishing houses love them. Streaming companies can't get enough of them.

Comedy. Drama. Think about those two words for a moment. In comedy, the hero goes on a journey and by the end of each episode has learned nothing. In drama, the exact opposite is true. How on earth is it possible to create a comedy drama? How do you write a script that manages to hold these two contradictory ideas in a single place?

The question matters for anyone who wants to add comedy to their dramatic story, or drama to their comedy.

It's important if you want to send a script to the BBC. Every year their Writing Department calls for comedy drama scripts. In a more recent and welcome development, the Comedy Department has sought to clarify exactly what it means by sitcom: broad big-laughs shows like Not Going Out, family comedy (Ghosts), young adult (People Just Do Nothing).

That's super helpful to us, especially at Sitcom Geeks where we've been seeking that kind of clarity for years. The BBC Comedy Department, as far as you're concerned, are looking for stand-alone sitcom episodes. Jokes. No story arcs. No learning, no hugs.

The first point to make is that there are far more similarities to comedy and drama than there are differences. As far as the legendary TV writer Steven Moffat is concerned, "comedy and drama are not different things." And he has a good piece of practical advice, which is to put a gag in the drama early to conceal a recurring plot point.

Everyone comes back to the same point we dealt with in Chapter Three - "the writer's voice". If you want to stand out in this fantastically over-crowded marketplace, you need to spend some deep time with yourself.

My former co-writer Paul McKenzie (now a TV producer) says "When I talk to writers, I rarely want bottom drawer pitches. I prefer to hear their life stories and see what interests them and me."

The best writing doesn't necessarily come from our personal suffering but there are sure to be stories from around your life – family relationships, history, personal life achievements and failures – that can be starting points for your drama. Start from reality but you can make the rest up – you are writing fiction after all. That reality is what initially draws an audience in, a key to defining 'your voice'.

Comedy-drama was the form I grew up loving most, without realising it. The great sitcoms of my childhood, Steptoe And Son, The Likely Lads, Dad's Army and others, grew out of the British theatre tradition. All had strong self-contained stories every episode.

My favourite writers in my teenage years were Alan Plater, Colin Welland, Willy Russell. They wrote laugh-out-loud plays in the 1970s, then became successful TV writers across comedy and drama. Jack Rosenthal flitted from sitcom to drama and back again without anyone taking him to task about the distinction. I loved his sitcoms The Dustbinmen and The Lovers as much as his classic one-off dramas like Barmitzvah Boy and P'Tang Yang Kipperbang.

We can partly answer the question "what is comedy-drama?" with – "it's whatever Steven Moffat writes." Simon Nye is another who enjoyed success writing sitcoms but is now in charge of ITV's comedy-drama The Durrells. Sally Wainwright has never, to my knowledge, written a sitcom but her dramas are packed with humour. Last Tango in Halifax is one of the funniest shows of the last few years, while even her gritty Happy Valley has moments of dark humour. Other writers who have mastered the form include Debbie Horsfield, Kay Mellor and Jack Thorne.

What is comedy drama? Given that everyone is talking about the composition with so many generalisations, I don't want to be too prescriptive here and say, "this is what you should do." Whatever stage you're at with your latest project, it's worth taking a step back and asking another question to add to the ones we've already discussed regarding who and what it's about:

Can I move the story forward without growing the main characters?

One of the mantras of this book is "sitcom characters learn nothing," I've already said it in this chapter, but I can't say it often enough. Sitcom characters learn nothing. Okay maybe that's too much for one chapter.

Watch an episode of Cold Feet though and you'll see that quite often by the end of the episode, one or two of the characters have changed almost imperceptibly. They'll come back next week and make the same mistakes, but this time they may do so while fully aware of the trouble it will get them into.

The question is how do *you* write comedy drama? How do you square the progression of a story and its dramatic call to action with the comedic flaw that suggests nothing will ever change?

The key to writing successful comedy drama is to focus not on the outcome, but the journey.

Just because comedy characters learn no lessons doesn't mean their stories are less gripping. Meanwhile a character who learns and grows in the final reel of the movie can still be a deluded idiot right up to that point. David Brent is the perfect example of this.

One other answer is to look at the series arc. I'm not saying it's the only answer, but it's one I've been thinking about and applying to my own ideas, and so far it has been helpful. I'll let you know how helpful once I've signed my own $100m deal with Netflix.

This is not something that requires great detail. Assuming that most of you reading this are British, you'll have in your mind the familiar template of the six-episode series. Before you start to write your instalment, give some thought to how the whole show is going to take place over that time.

Very broadly speaking, episode one will introduce your world and the people who inhabit it, and episode six will involve one or more of those people in a climactic story that will leave your audience wondering, ideally desperate to know, what will happen next.

You don't have to have travelled too far in time over that period. If a series represents a year in the life of your protagonist, the narrative arc allows you to map out even the most mundane of stories with drama. A school year maybe, like each of the Harry Potter books. A newlywed couple, or someone newly divorced. A year in a new job. All you're looking for is a big way to introduce them, a big way to conclude the story (allowing for audiences to speculate on how it will continue) and four episodes in between.

Maurice Gran, who as one half of Marks and Gran knows a thing or two about comedy, drama and comedy drama, says "Drama often demands drastic and massive character changes. Not actually that realistic. Comedy allows characters to change and develop more gradually and subtly. Nevertheless, comedy is still a form of drama."

Once you start to develop those middle episodes, you can go back to thinking of them as self-contained. At this point you don't need to know which is episode 2, 3, 4 or 5. If you're following a year in the life of a married couple, once you know roughly where you want them to be at the end of episode six the other stories should slot into place fairly straightforwardly.

If they're already on the verge of splitting up by the end of the series, that gives you a sense of the tone of say, episode two, where everything is still relatively sweet and light, and episode five where that endearing laugh that first attracted you to him is seriously beginning to grate.

And that leaves your middle two episodes, and you can imagine stories where characters try and get something they can't have, or fail to see themselves as others do, or try to fulfil a need that can't be met, all within a self-contained episode.

You may find as you're writing these characters, who you have only recently created and brought to life, that they are taking you somewhere you weren't expecting. That's okay at this stage. It can take a whole series for an actor and writer to come together and find exactly who the character is. Leslie Knope is a great example of someone who is very different at the start of season two of Parks & Rec, to the person she was at the start of season one.

Don't plan your series arc in so much detail that you find yourself deep into the script, squeezing your character into a story that won't fit. At this stage you're easing your character into the world like a new-born baby, let the character help *you* find where they're going.

SUMMARY

How do you create comedy-drama? In comedy no one learns and grows from their mistakes. Learning and growing is literally the key to drama.

You can find ways round this. Characters can learn from their mistakes, but return to make them again later on. Just like we do in real life.

Characters can change imperceptibly. Have an idea where you want them to be at the start of episode one and the end of episode six. Whichever episode you choose to write, you'll know where the character is on their journey.

As you're creating new characters, allow the story to help mould them.

18
Activate – Escalate – Resolve

Let's pause for a moment and remind ourselves that we're doing this for fun. Stop what you're doing. I mean, don't stop reading this specifically, read this first, then stop, otherwise you won't know what to do next.

Go for a walk. Look at the trees. Marvel at the gifts of nature. Try not to think too hard about what we're doing to it.

Give yourself a pat on the back for having got this far. We are often the harshest critics of our own work. Apart from the bloke who gave my Edinburgh show a one-star review in 1978 but it's only been 45 years, so I'm sure I'll get over it soon.

Creating something new is a massive challenge. Most people don't even try. Some who do give up after a while. The obstacles may seem too great. To paraphrase Michael Rosen, when you come to an obstacle that you can't go over, under or around, you need to go through it.

The answer won't always come while you're staring anxiously at the blinking cursor on the blank screen. Take a break. Stretch. Breathe in. And out.

Okay back to work.

If you've ever responded to a BBC Writersroom call-out for scripts, you'll know that one of the things they ask for is "that something special that makes us want to read more."

This is all that any writer can hope for: that our stories be interesting enough to keep the reader engaged. It's one of the main reasons that human beings survive, and why there will always be a demand for stories: everyone wants to know what's going to happen next.

It could be a fiendishly complicated fraud scam on Brooklyn 99 involving the FBI, the CIA and Doug Judy. Or John and

Kayleigh driving to and from work in Car Share. How will Peralta and Santiago catch the criminal? How will John get one step closer to declaring his love for Kayleigh? When we love our shows, we are deeply invested in the characters. The story doesn't need to be big to move us emotionally.

One thing I'm certain about is that whatever happens over the course of your sitcom, movie, novel or magnum opus, every episode or chapter should have its own self-contained story. That's true in comedy and in drama, so it should also be true in comedy-drama.

We need to remind ourselves of this frequently. I do, for sure because I often forget my own mantra. The overall premise of the show is not the same thing as this week's episode. I'll write it again, and still forget it. The overall premise of the show is not the same thing as this week's episode.

You don't have to bring the whole story to its end in a single episode or chapter, but you do need to start and complete at least one major affair. For this to happen you need three things to ensure that this week's instalment works:

Activate

Escalate

Resolve

Each of these corresponds to each of Aristotle's Three Acts. Now let's take Syd's Mathematical Field and plough it into a short document. Something between 300 and 400 words.

Confining ourselves to a single episode of your series, or the full synopsis of your longer piece, we **activate** the main story in the opening lines. A big thing happens, hopefully a proactive move by your main protagonist, that has consequences. This will take up a paragraph, maybe 50 or so words.

As the story develops the protagonist will respond. Each time it pushes the action to a more perilous place and the story **escalates,** one step at a time, to a moment around three quarters of the way through where **all is lost** or won for your protagonist. This is the bulk of your document, Act Two. 150-200 words.

You have just a quarter of the text or less remaining to **resolve** that. Another 50-100 words.

The above has clarity and an almost poetic simplicity, so much so that I barely need to explain. But I'll try. Remember your characters are driving the story. And, unless you're involved in national politics, every action has a consequence.

Here's an unoriginal flat-share comedy drama I'm writing for the sake of this exercise:

Activate – start your story, preferably in the opening five pages of your script. The housemates Anne and Betty have a guest coming to stay – it's Anne's long lost cousin Cath from Australia. Anne hates her.

Escalate – Cath comes to stay and gets on well with Betty.

As a consequence, Anne is annoyed. She tries to warn Betty that Cath is not all she seems.

As a consequence, Betty confides in Cath that Anne doesn't like her.

As a consequence, Cath turns on the charm and gradually drives a wedge between Anne and Betty that goes so deep that

As a consequence, Anne and Betty fall out.

That's it. Note the escalation of the drama. From a small disagreement, we quickly get to the place where Anne and Betty are never going to talk again. All is lost.

It's not exactly Dickens but it's a story, and it has escalated to the point where if things get any worse Anne and Betty will split up, and my comedy drama will be over.

Resolve – this was Cath's plan all along. She's broke and needs somewhere to live, so she was hoping to force Betty out. Then she could move in rent free with her cousin. Rumbled somehow by Anne and Betty, they plot together and flush her out, Cath disappears, equilibrium is restored.

The story is as generic as they come, but in the episode, it comes close to the two main people in the show never talking to each other again. You can't just arrive at that moment, you must build to it, raise the stakes, so we reach a point close to the end of the show where all is lost (or for Cath, all is won).

That episode has drama - Anne and Betty are about to fall out - and comedy: resolution, the equilibrium of their relationship is restored and phew, we can laugh again. I may be working towards a situation at the end of the series where Anne and Betty are in major conflict. I've resolved their differences for now, but given a glimpse of where the cracks might be in the friendship. That's all the series arc comedy drama I need at this stage.

My little plot there has come in at around 200 words. It's the bare bones of the story. You might want to add a few embellishments.

I would probably set up more of the relationship between Anne and Betty in my opening. Where their friendship currently stands. There may already be some underlying tension. I'd want to add more detail to the middle Act Two section, be sure that both Anne and Betty are being proactive. They are, after all, my main characters, not Cath. I think the resolve section is correct at this stage.

Once you have a rough sense of where your story is going, and you're happy that your main characters are driving the story, not the other way round, you're almost ready to start writing that script.

Before we take our final step in the pre-script stage, there are two things I must remind you of.

First, be careful not to become embroiled in a plot that stubbornly refuses to resolve itself through the actions of the characters. If the plot is doing all the work, then there's something wrong with the characters. Fix that now, while you still have plenty of time.

And the last point, not sure if I've mentioned this before, but the overall premise of this show is not the same thing as this week's episode.

SUMMARY

Begin plotting your story with a short document, around 3-400 words.

It should mirror Aristotle's Three Act model. Act One – Activate. Act Two – Escalate. Act Three – Resolve.

Be sure to have an all-is-lost moment at the end of the escalation.

If you're writing an episode as part of a series, remember this is not the same thing as the show's premise.

19

The Art of The Outline – Tell Don't Show

We're almost ready to turn all that hard work you've done up to now into a first draft.

Between working out what's going to happen and putting it on paper or screen, you need one last step.

When we're helping new writers develop their scripts, we sometimes mention things that we assume writers already know. We say things like "write an outline" without explaining what that means.

I struggled at school, where most subjects were taught through the dissemination of facts that required astounding feats of memory. Measuring volume, the Battle of Bosworth Field, the absorption of biological processes into my brain by osmosis – teachers spouted the data and left us to fill the gaps.

What do I mean by an outline?

It's been hard to separate out each part of the process. Hopefully the journey is clearer now. We began with the idea, or the premise. Moved on to the characters and the world they live in. Started to think of lots of episode stories, concentrated on developing a shorter selection of these. Didn't confuse the episode with the premise.

You have narrowed down your choice to one story – the one you will turn into a full-length work.

As you develop this, be sure it still ties in with the idea, world and characters you have come up with. Have a look at those 25 words again. Have they changed? Almost certainly. Update them.

In the outline you're going to state what happens in every scene, and how what takes place in that scene will lead you into the next scene. This is part of what BBC Writersroom are referring to when they ask that your writing keeps them engaged.

Will Storr's excellent book The Science of Storytelling describes this process well: "Every scene in a compelling story is a cause that triggers a childlike curiosity about its potential effects – a relentless adhering to forward motion, one thing leading to another."

As the action escalates you will reach a point, about three quarters of the way through, where all is lost (or won) for your main character.

As you're writing it, you're staying true to the overall premise of your idea, illustrating the "what's it really about" aspect of it. And the flawed characters you have created are going to take actions that will get them deeper into trouble.

Before you get to the exciting part of fun and jokery, you must write the boring bit. If you want ice cream for pudding, you're going to have to eat that broccoli first.

The outline, in very simple terms, is an instruction manual you are writing, mostly for you, entitled How to Write My Episode. It's the second most important document, the last thing before you finally sit down to write write rather than just write, so it's important to get it precise.

We often talk about a script having to adhere to the instruction "show don't tell." In other words, in a script it is the actions of the character that move the story forward, not the things they say. We need to see the results of the character's errors with our eyes.

With an outline the reverse is true. In an outline, the instruction is "tell don't show."

Del Boy falling through the opening of a bar is one of the funniest moments in sitcom history. If you disagree, that's only because you've seen it too many times.

Imagine writing that scene. When you think of it you know it's going to be funny. But before you get to that stage you have to write it down in a way that will convey why.

"In this scene Del Boy is trying to impress a girl, but only ends up falling into a bar."

Remember this is not a document for the audience, it's your guide to make sure you keep track of where your story is heading.

Here's what that scene might look like in an outline:

Del Boy and Trigger have gone to a club to pick up women. Del is near the bar, explaining to Trigger what he needs to do to attract their attention. While he's talking a member of staff leaves the bar and leaves the bar hatch open as they go to collect some glasses.

Del boy sees a woman across the room giving him a look and he tells Trigger to act cool. He leans back casually but there is nothing to lean back on as the bar is open, and he falls into the bar.

Don't worry that this reads like an IKEA instruction manual for putting together your Billy bookcase. At this stage you don't want anything more elaborate. Save that for the script. Watch the scene again and you'll see the embellishments. The writer John Sullivan has built Del Boy's smug confidence in the dialogue with Trigger. David Jason has added the kind of physical humour that made him a comedy superstar.

It took me 95 words to describe that minute and a half of action. You can see why this document is going to be long.

Initially you want to write out each plot separately. Your main plot – the A plot - will probably be around two thirds of the whole. Generally, sitcoms have one or two smaller plots – B and C plots. These help to keep all your characters in play and vary the pace of the show to add tension or laughs to the main story.

When you have all the plots written you need to meld them together to create a whole. B plots usually start a bit later.

Because you're probably writing something new, you'll be tempted to open with backstory. I would try to avoid this as much as possible. You can tell a lot about a fictional creation by giving them something to do very early on. Or put them with another character and we'll quickly learn a lot about status. You can show us which person is trying harder to please the other, whether that one is calm or tense, stuffy or cool, cautious or impulsive.

Be conscious of everything you're putting in there. Make sure everything happens for a reason. Why is every scene there?

Imagine your outline in terms of creating a new house.

You've spent every moment up to now getting the foundations ready. Premise, story, world creation, characters. I'm looking at the space where the house will go and there's still nothing to see yet. But you have built the foundations.

Now it's time to look at the architect's blueprint. What are you trying to do with this house? That's all part of the process. These rooms go here, that window there, and I want the brickwork to be a different colour here and here. I can see it in my head but need to convey all that to the architect. They must pass that knowledge onto the builder.

When the house is built, and the brickwork is the same colour everywhere, that's because I wasn't clear enough at the outline stage about what I wanted to happen.

It's always easier to fix in the outline stage. Be clear about what needs to happen in every moment of every scene.

For the only time when you're creating your story, tell don't show.

SUMMARY

The outline is a necessary document before you start your first draft.

You're going to explain what will happen in each scene. And how the consequence of the end of one scene plays out at the start of the next one.

No flourishes. No clever word play. Just the facts.

Everything needs to be there for a reason. If it's not revealing character, or moving the story on, then bin it.

Imagine this document to be the architect's blueprint. You've built the foundations, now you're showing the architect – your writer self – how to build the draft.

Part Four
Writing

Finally.

Apologies for taking this long to get to the point. I hope you appreciate why it's worth holding back as long as you can before diving in.

I know many writers prefer to start and see where that takes them, but I think when you're starting out it's helpful to have some structure in place. If, never having run before, you were thinking of doing a marathon, would you get out of your chair this minute and see if you could manage it first time?

The first three parts of this book have been all about preparation. The next three are about execution.

I have, pleasingly, reached the exact midpoint of the book. As John Yorke explains in Into the Woods, I'm at the place where the understanding of your quest has become clear.

Time to run headfirst towards those obstacles in your way.

20

Say It Again, Sam

Writing, without giving away too much of the plot in this gripping chronicle of learning how to write comedy, is re-writing. And there'll be more about that shortly.

I re-read this book last year and realised there was more – and less – to say. "How to write dialogue" was a crucial omission.

Recently one of our regular Sitcom Geeks listeners asked: "When you write dialogue how do you circumvent the classic problem of 'the characters are talking to the audience, not each other'?"

Coincidentally this listener has also been a guest on the show: Alex Garrick-Wright, one half of the winning team in our 2020 Write A Scene competition. Which if I remember had great dialogue. Even the best writers are working hard to get better.

When we're creating a new show, we tend to put dialogue to one side. There are so many other things that must be worked out ahead: theme, character, story, the world we're creating. And it's taken this long to get to this chapter.

Which doesn't mean it's not important. Unless you're Jed Mercurio, who actually says "Dialogue is the least important part of my writing." Which is fair enough when you think that a typical Jed Mercurio scene is ten seconds of people talking and five minutes of heart-stopping, stomach-churning tension and action.

For comedy writers, removing one vowel tells us that "dialogue is the *last* important part of my writing." Not entirely true but sod it, I thought that was quite a clever observation so it's staying.

Visual jokes are a vital component of comedy and we'll be coming to them shortly as well, but dialogue is a crucial part of what we do.

What do we mean by dialogue? I've identified four key qualities.

First, and most important, dialogue is **character.** Think of the last conversation you had with someone. How much were you being your true self? We're all putting on a show a lot of the time.

What your hero or heroine says tells the audience who they are. David Brent believes it when he tells us he's a chilled-out entertainer. He even knows how to play guitar. We watch and respond: "Oh no this is how you see yourself. It's a disaster for you."

Our creations above all lack self-awareness. If they had it, they wouldn't say that.

Second, it's about what isn't said. Frequently referred to as **subtext.** In every scene in a sitcom, at least one of the characters wants something. Too often I read scripts where character A enters and asks character B for something. And the answer is either yes or no. End of drama.

Again, you need to think about how you approach people in real life when you want something. And exaggerate it.

For instance, I might fancy a takeaway curry for supper tonight. I know that my wife would prefer Vietnamese. I wouldn't start the conversation "I want a takeaway curry tonight". Instead, devious soul I am, I'd draw attention to the new restaurant that's opened round the corner, regardless of what they sell. Gradually I'll draw the conversation round to saying: "that's given me a sudden craving for a curry."

You big liar Dave, there was no suddenness at all, you were scheming from the moment you began that chat. Everybody lies. We know that if we start with our truth, it's not going to persuade the other person to do things our way.

The third reason for dialogue is **exposition.** Occasionally you need to convey important information. There's no getting round it, and if you make the actual dialogue too funny the audience may miss the vital story moment you're trying to get across.

Still, it must be used sparingly. If you're going to have it, find a way to make the context funny. In the Austin Powers movies, the Q character is called Basil Exposition, which allows us to learn the information while enjoying the joke.

In sitcom, our protagonists never learn, and stories reset at the beginning of each episode. But even if you're writing a movie or comedy drama, you might be surprised at how little exposition you need. Big chunks of dialogue need to be broken up. Avoid them altogether if you can.

There are a couple of other ways to get round the exposition problem. First you might decide to have a narrator. But be careful, there have been so many versions of this that you need to find new ways of using them. I read a lot of scripts where the narration is so intricate and central to the story that I wonder if the writer should consider turning it into a short story or a novel.

Another way is turning your show into a mockumentary. Personally, I have a real issue with these. The original mockumentary – "rockumenatary, if you will" – was the movie Spinal Tap, which was made more than 40 years ago. In my opinion, nothing has improved on that, although UK Office comes close.

The form allows you to do all the above - use subtext, lie, tell story, reveal character – because the payoff can be instant: a quick pan of the camera revealing the opposite of what's being said.

I'm not saying: "don't write mockumentary scripts." Especially since last time I said it in a podcast, two weeks later the BBC announced that their next flagship family sitcom would be a mockumentary.

If you can find a way of doing it that doesn't mimic The Office or Spinal Tap, give it a try. What We Do in The Shadows comes close, although I think of that more as a new take on comedy horror than as mockumentary.

In Modern Family it's used sparingly, like punctuation, to vary the pace of the episode and bring light and shade to the characters. I saw a lot of mockumentary scripts in our Sitcom Contest last year and too often it felt like every punchline to every joke was the same.

The final responsibility of dialogue is to move the story on or **clarify** what just happened. Especially at the start of a new scene. This is given special attention in American comedy shows, which are interrupted by adverts every few minutes. Seinfeld became the masters of this domain, returning to Jerry's flat to re-live the pre ad-break moments in a kind of funny, rhythmic singalong.

You can bring further insight to your characters. That was a terrible date your lead character went on. We all saw it. Next scene they say: "I think the date went very well."

I was thinking of adding a fifth feature, which is jokes. But these should be a consequence of everything happening in those other four situations. Jokes that come from nowhere in a narrative sitcom are not narrative sitcom, they're stand-up. People sparring funny lines across each other is rarely funny outside of a panel show.

What don't we mean by dialogue? I have identified four key quandaries.

The first of these is *monologue*. Scripts often appear on my screen displaying huge slabs of type. Even if you're writing a novel, that lack of white space denoting new paragraphs tells me I'm going to have to take a deep breath and dive in to keep track of the story.

The rhythm of comedy, to quote the title of one of Rob Long's memoirs is "Set up. Joke. Set up. Joke." Which is a slight exaggeration. But we want to laugh at every joke. Think of that white space as the pause between savouring what's just gone and getting ready for the new thought that's coming.

If you insist on having Sadie deliver a three-minute speech to her work colleagues, at least let's have some fun around it. Cut away to a couple of workmates snickering in the corner, or a power-point that goes wrong, or the tea trolley arriving.

Next is *conversation*. Listen to people talking. Most of it is boring. Or all over the place. "How's your back today?" "Bit better than yesterday thanks." "What shall we have for dinner tonight?" "Did you have a good sleep?" We repeat stuff. Jump from one subject to another.

John Yorke defines dialogue as "the illusion of conversation." Dialogue is artifice. It has to be like conversation. Our lives are repetitive, TV is recognisably like real life, but it's compressed. It resembles reality.

The third problem is *recollection*. I see this all the time, even in shows I love. "Do you remember that time we went to the swimming pool?"... "Please don't do that thing again with your lip, you know it drives me mad.".... "How many times have I told you not to stick your little sister's fingers in the toaster?"

This is the kind of problem Alex's question is referring to. Are they talking to each other or the audience? If you're writing these lines, it means you don't yet know enough about what makes your leads funny. Maybe you don't believe in them enough yet.

These lines take you out of the scene. How do you avoid them? Make sure something is happening. Try and express this thought visually. More often than not, the key is to read it out loud and listen to yourself. You'll hear the inauthenticity of it, and you'll probably end up cutting it.

Trust the audience. Let them do some of the work. Tell them "Here's two plus two." Let them work out the rest of the sum.

Finally, I see too many scenes that begin like an athletics race. "On your marks... get set... wait for it..." *Come into your scene as late as possible.* Our natural inclination is to start things first thing in the morning. It's completely understandable. But not necessary. You can convey someone arriving late for work without having them sleeping through the alarm, gulping down breakfast, missing the bus. Why not open the scene at the office? Meeting's already begun. Hero arrives dishevelled, wearing odd shoes. We get it.

Like the angry email you compose but don't send to the boss, sometimes you have to write this filler to get it out of your system.

What else can you do to make your dialogue zing along? Prepare. Before you write the scene, work out: what is your character hoping to get from this interaction? What is the person they're talking to hoping to get? What will they end up with? Watch out for a character in the scene just being reactive. Give both characters an agenda. What is the purpose of this scene? If the scene hasn't moved the story on it should be cut. Keep referring to your outline.

Once you've got across everything you need to move the story on, you need to get out big and fast. End the scene with a big joke. Imagine this scene or chapter is an audience sitcom. Do you want to end your scene with 300 people sitting in silence?

Which would you rather hear at this point – gales of laughter?

Or the Eastenders theme? Doof doof, doof doof doof. I know what I'm having.

SUMMARY

Dialogue is about revealing character.

It's as much about what people are not saying as what they're saying.

Dialogue revealing backstory should be kept to a minimum.

And it needs to move the story on.

Dialogue is not monologue.

Dialogue is not like normal conversation. It's the *illusion* of conversation.

Dialogue needs to avoid defining characters by telling the audience about things they have never witnessed.

Dialogue should be cut, ruthlessly. Come into the scene as late as you can.

21

A Man Walks into A Joke

Jokes. Jokes, jokes, jokes, jokes, jokes. It's pretty obvious isn't it? If you want to write comedy you have to be able to write jokes. That's most of what you should be writing, most of the time. If you're writing stand-up comedy, or topical gags, and the last sentence you wrote wasn't funny, then either the next sentence must be, or you'll have to cut them both.

It's amazing how often comedy writers forget to write jokes. Even the most experienced professionals – maybe swept up with the excitement of communicating their great new idea or absorbed by the story they want to tell – sometimes forget that they are being paid to write comedy. Comedy means that people should be laughing nearly all the time. When they're not laughing it's because they're listening to the set-up for the next laugh.

Entire scripts are developed, through several drafts, overseen by producers and TV commissioners and made into full programmes before anyone clocks that one of the main problems is there aren't enough jokes.

I'm not making a qualitative judgement here, but a quantitative one. The jokes I like may not be the ones you do, but there should be lots of them. If you're writing a scene and struggling to find a way to fit some jokes around your narrative or characters, then there's something wrong in that scene with your narrative or characters. The solution will hardly ever involve sacrificing jokes.

And if you're writing a show that you're not expecting to be filmed in front of an audience, that makes no difference. Shows like Bluestone 42, Brooklyn 99 and Grace and Frankie are as packed full of jokes as any number of audience sitcoms.

Why does so much TV comedy fail to live up to our expectations? Or if it's something you've written, why does the show you're watching on the screen look inferior to the one you were carrying for months in your head? It's usually because the characters or the story have not been sufficiently well-defined. Not enough jokes may not be the cause of your problem, but it will often be the effect.

One of the great problems with jokes is you never know if they're going to work until you try them out.

The commonest mistake made by beginner stand-ups is to be thrown when the audience fails to laugh at their jokes. The performer delivers what they think is a funny line, and the audience doesn't laugh. The audience aren't judging the performer at this point, as far as they know they're still building up to the joke. The performer is thinking: "They didn't laugh at that line! That's my favourite joke. They hate me."

Their demeanour on stage starts to reflect this, now the audience see the look of panic and start to lose confidence. They weren't being judgmental before, but they are now. It's a self-fulfilling prophecy because the performer didn't have the experience to ride through the lack of laughs and move on as if nothing wrong had happened.

An experienced performer will try the joke again at other gigs, maybe tweak it, add a word or sentence here, move it around, put it in a different place in a routine. Find a way to make it work or finally, ditch it. The great comedian and gag writer Gary Delaney can even explain why a joke that made them roar in Runcorn will tank in Telford.

Why do so many comedy writers work in pairs? If you can make the person sitting next to you laugh, then at least one person aside from you has found it funny.

Every professional writer has a list of jokes they loved that never made it into the final script. Or failed to get a laugh on the night: American comedy writers even have a lovely name for this – "the new restaurant on the corner." It can't possibly fail, it's approachable from two different roads, it has potential to attract double the number of customers – but check your local high street, that restaurant on the corner is always the first business to close.

Then again, you may have dashed off a few lines that get the biggest laughs of the episode. As American sitcom writer Fred Barron says, "Life isn't always fair, but sometimes it's unfair in your favour."

"Slippery customers, jokes", as Uncle Jimmy might have said in an episode of Reggie Perrin. Researching this chapter, I found that there's hardly anything written anywhere defining jokes. Stand-up comic Sally Holloway has written a great manual for comedy writers, The Serious Guide to Joke Writing. And there's plenty of scientific and psychological analysis of why we laugh, including The Naked Jape by Lucy Greeves and Jimmy Carr, whose thoughtful narrative is nicely punctuated by hundreds of gags.

American writer Joe Toplyn can show you in detail how to write gags for late night American talk show hosts. But there are hardly any specific definitions of jokes.

One of the few items on the internet refers to "mathematical jokes" as a new category. I'd say that's a little niche, but music and mathematics are closely related to joke creation. A joke is like an equation, where set-up + unexpected twist = punchline. And the rhythm of poetry and music beats through the heart of all great comedy. Seinfeld is the best example of this, where many new scenes open with a précis of the last one, and it sounds like they're singing.

What is a joke?

A joke is a three-act story. All stories have three acts, you know this because I keep banging on about Aristotle and The Poetics.

A man walks into a bar. What would Aristotle make of this?

A man walks into a bar. There's your Act One, it's the real world, nothing unusual about that. But there's something I haven't told you about him – he's wearing a suit made of bread and has a tomato on his head, which you will admit is unusual. That's our inciting incident. Farewell to the real world of Act One, where men walk into bars and it's no big deal. We're about to go on a fantastic journey to Act Two, to a new world where sure, men walk into bars like before, but now they go in wearing suits made of bread and have tomatoes on their heads.

You're coming with for now, this notion is outlandish, but you're prepared to suspend your disbelief because "a man walks into a bar" has alerted you to the possibility that the end of this story may make you laugh. In a movie this will lead to around an hour of complications, but because this is a ten-second joke we only get one complication, which is that the barman gets cross and asks him to leave.

You may not have been expecting that, either. The barman has raised the stakes, and we have reached the point of maximum jeopardy, the end of Act Two. What is going to happen to our hero? Will he stay, and face the consequences of an angry barman, or leave, unable to satisfy his alcoholic cravings? It's time for the second twist, when our bread-suited hero decides he has to understand the reasons for the barman's anger. "Why?" he beseeches the barman, "why must I leave?"

The barman points to a sign above the bar, which provides the answer, Act Three, the punchline. The sign says, "we don't serve sandwiches."

I accept this isn't the funniest joke you've ever heard, some might say it's not even a joke, it's a pun, and puns aren't jokes. Tell that to Twitter, and to the hundreds and thousands of Milton Jones and Tim Vine fans.

But it should alert you to the component parts required to make a joke funny – even as you're aware that the guaranteed way to kill a joke is to break it down into its component parts.

Enjoy your next stand-up show and pray that I'm not sitting next to you in the audience, holding a flip chart.

SUMMARY

It's hard to know if a joke will work until you try it out on someone. This is why it helps if you write with a partner.

Every joke is a Three Act story. Movies are Three Act stories that last 90 minutes, Jokes last around 10 seconds but follow the same pattern.

Act One – set up. Activating incident. Act Two – complication, all is lost. Act Three – resolution and punchline.

22

This Chapter Contains Every Joke You'll Ever Write

As well as there being hardly any information available to answer the question "what is a joke?" there's even less defining different types. I remember as a kid being aware of the accepted wisdom that "there are only seven jokes", which was probably said as a joke, but anyone old enough to remember The Benny Hill Show and Seaside Special may be forgiven for thinking that was an overestimate.

This isn't an exhaustive list, but it's what I've come up with based on my own observations. I've defined six broad types, one fewer than above, but then I'm sure whoever said there were seven jokes only did so because at that time seven was a funny number. (For a while the comedy number was 17, but that's been over-used, although 42 remains a staple thanks to Douglas Adams. Why are some numbers funnier than others? I don't know, I'm a joke writer not a numerologist.)

I'm sure there is a more detailed list to be written. Consider this as the opening conversation, the first attempts to answer the question "What kind of joke am I?"

1. Turns reality on its head

George Orwell described every joke as "a tiny revolution", and it is this, which can also be described as "surprise", that is one of the most effective ways in which jokes work. Without wishing to be too dry about it, this joke sets you up to think something will happen, but then the unexpected occurs. "Gasp!" Spitting Image writer Stuart Silver used to proclaim in mock triumph when coming up with a joke, "It isn't this thing, it's another thing!"

Also included here is the reversal gag – the first of its kind was said to be from Rowan and Martin's Laugh-In, when a comedy Eastern European character said "I love America, here everybody watches television. In my country television watches you." Not bad for 1967.

I should also introduce you at this point to the "Langdon", named after the late great John Langdon, a prolific gag writer best known for his work with Rory Bremner. John may not have been the first but was certainly the best at putting two elements into the set-up of a joke, while making the punchline about the element you weren't expecting.

A recent example might have been "Boris Johnson has spoken out against the European Union's refusal to renegotiate his Northern Ireland protocol. Unwieldy, incompetent and disliked by millions, Mr Johnson..." Pause, sit back, and wait for the gales of laughter.

2. Recognition

This is the opposite of turning reality on its head. It gives you the reality you always knew - but took a comedy writer to point out. The best impressionists capture recognisable traits in famous voices and with only the smallest exaggeration make them funny. Many stand-ups begin their routines of comedy recognition with a rhetorical question, like when Jerry Seinfeld talks about betting on the horses – "Do the horses even know they're in a race?"

3. "Strained tension into nothing"

Thanks to comedy writer Robin Flavell for pointing this one out to me; a quotation from the 18th century German philosopher Immanuel Kant. Not a funny man himself although his surname never fails to raise a childish chuckle.

The Latin word that best describes these jokes is "bathos", which means anti-climactic. It's the kind of line that may follow the unwarranted boasts of a pompous fool. You might call that schadenfreude – enjoying someone getting their comeuppance.

Bathos is not to be confused with "pathos", which means deserving of our sympathy – but I think pathos is also relevant here. I love the word "strained" in that quote. This definition for me brings to mind those moments after great pathos in sitcoms like Frasier and Only Fools and Horses. When the next joke comes it's greeted with an explosive laugh of relief.

The "monster" sitcom character also features here. These are characters with no self-awareness, and we talk of pricking their pomposity, in the way you might pop a balloon. Kant's definition is apt here and applies frequently to David Brent.

I'd include in here jokes that make fun of tragedy. In the days before Twitter, it was incredibly shocking to hear jokes about famous people within hours of them dying. These days the best (and sickest) jokes will have been written, stolen, and retweeted before half the population even know the person had RIP-ed. Humour in the face of immediate tragedy is a coping mechanism, a way of dealing with the outpouring of grief we feel when someone we love dies.

Or the twisted expressions of an evil comic mind if you prefer.

4. Unpredictable

This is closely related to the first category, rather than turn reality on its head takes it in a new direction. The obvious word to use to describe these would be "surreal".

Be careful – starting a joke about a bicycle and making the punchline a fish rarely works unless there is some very un-surreal foundation to it. The outlandish comedy of Vic & Bob and The Mighty Boosh succeeds because it is rooted firmly in their extremely familiar comedy relationships.

Silly jokes, word play, puns, knock-knock, innuendo – anything that subverts our language. And repetition. If a joke's worth saying once, it's worth saying once.

5. Satire

Often taken these days to mean "Jokes about what's in the news", satire is one of our oldest joke forms and its strict definition is an attack, usually in verse, on authority and power.

Nowadays it's best described as a chance to let off steam, proof that in our democracy it's possible to mock the strong and powerful and not be killed, as still happens in some parts of the world. By the way, I've been writing topical comedy for more than 35 years and I'm afraid I can conclusively reveal that no joke has ever brought down a government.

6. Cruelty

This encompasses a large collection of joke types I don't need to define, do I? Mocking people's flaws and weaknesses, attacking those who are already weak, poking fun, bullying, all kinds of things the likes of you and I are far too cultured and urbane to attempt. You probably think you know exactly what I'm talking about, but you might be wrong.

There's plenty of room in this category for the racist anger of those who still carry Bernard Manning's torch (and wear his hood), and the cruelty of Jimmy Carr towards travellers and the disabled. Jokes attacking women are back in the mainstream – though people who think they are edgy doing rape jokes need to be reminded that in the 1970s, those were the kind of gags you could find in BBC1 family sitcoms.

Cruelty in humour goes way beyond this. We all like cruel humour, more than we might be prepared to admit. What's so funny about someone falling over in the street? It's probably happened to you, and it might have been really painful. I knew a man, a friend of my parents, who broke his leg after tripping over a paving stone in the street.

And go on, admit it, you're suppressing the urge to laugh even though I've just written a sentence about someone breaking their leg after falling over in the street.

Denis Norden said that nearly all jokes could be defined as "an unexpected withholding of sympathy."

Satire, surprise, recognition, he saw this element of cruelty in every joke. "It happens when your sense of humanity demands that there should be sympathy – and sympathy is unexpectedly withdrawn."

There are other things to consider when writing jokes – the status and position of the person telling them, the use of rhythm and word play as mentioned, taking imaginative and tangential leaps. But I think these are issues around the joke.

Have I missed any joke forms? Any joke forms at all? Might there indeed be seven? Oh yes. Number seven: repetition.

SUMMMARY

There are several types of joke – turn reality on its head, recognition, anti-climax, unpredictability, satire, cruelty and repetition.

Almost every joke fits into Denis Norden's definition of "a momentary removal of sympathy."

One type of joke I haven't mentioned yet – repetition.

23
Joking in Character

Every so often there's a review of a TV show (invariably in The Guardian) that says something like "this is such a great comedy and one of the reasons is that they don't bother with jokes." I exaggerate for comic effect, but not much.

You should see us comedy writers when we all pile into our Comedy Writers' Page on Facebook to slag off this latest nonsense by some skittish young reviewer straight out of college who's been allowed to write this crap. We're hilarious.

"Oh really?" we say "It's a good comedy without jokes is it? Remind me next time I go to the fishmonger, to say to him 'I'm sorry I'm no longer coming here, from now on I'll be going to the local hardware store, it's a great fishmonger because they don't bother with fish, anyway this notion you have of *selling fish* is so outmoded, and another thing the hardware store smells a damn sight nicer.'"

We know what these Guardian critics mean, of course, we're not idiots. For more than 20 years we've been watching the gradual transformation of TV comedy from studio-based sitcom with a laughing audience to location-based stories directed by wannabe movie makers.

Anyone under 30 is far more used to receiving their narrative comedy without the backing track of a cackling bunch of idiots "that's obviously been dubbed on after to show us where to laugh." It hasn't, but that particular hill on which I continue to die is for another time.

What these critics are saying is, they watched The Office then Peep Show, proper funny shows that looked like drama. They enjoyed those mega-budget American dramas with heavy doses of humour and irony like Breaking Bad and Better Call Saul. And decided that all British comedy should try and be like that, with a fraction of the budget and no teams of writers.

The other thing they're saying is they no longer enjoy the rhythm of narrative comedy. As I have frequently pointed out, comedy is like music. We instinctively listen to verses that are like set-ups to jokes, and expect chorus hooks like we expect punchlines, and we particularly like big endings. Like the funniest joke that comes at the end of a stand-up routine, which in its entirety usually lasts about as long as a pop song. Leave that to the comedians, the critics are saying, keeping that rhythm for a funny story no longer feels normal.

It's a long, old tradition that started with Greek comedy. It continued through to Shakespeare, then pantomime, music hall, end-of-the-pier show, and to audience sitcom. You hear laughter as the rhythm of comedy, increased by the shared experience of being in the room when it happens. Apart from in the form of stand-up or panel show, that way of experiencing comedy has become unfashionable.

I've spent years resisting this argument but am starting to wonder if I need to address this elephant in the comedy writers' room.

The show that made me challenge my prejudices was Fleabag. I enjoyed both series, but remembered a moment from the first, a short scene in which, while the boyfriend unable to bring her to orgasm nipped off to the loo, she watched a speech by the super handsome President Obama to help her finish the job.

The boyfriend came back, was angry when he saw what had happened, and stormed out. "That's a funny set-up idea," I thought, because comedy writers rarely sit and laugh at stuff, we're too busy analysing it. "The scene that follows will be hilarious. We'll see two characters coming to terms with their relationship falling apart because this bloke can't abide having his masculinity threatened by the President of the USA."

Although I carried on enjoying the show, I remember being slightly disappointed that the scene in my head never happened. The bloke ran off, and we rarely saw him again.

I thought little more of this until Fleabag started to become that rare thing, a breakout hit. It built a bigger audience beyond the comedy world, was adored by the media and won loads of awards. The Obama scene became the clip that went viral.

What I had wanted from that scene was an exploration of relationships from what in my mind I expect of a show that is advertised as a comedy. It was made with money earmarked "Comedy Department" – but that's not what Fleabag was ever meant to be. It was always about Fleabag, her own self-obsession, and the self-destructive path she was going down. Sometimes it would be funny, sometimes not. You, the audience, had to take it or leave it on those terms.

And for the first time, the observation that "you don't need jokes for a comedy show to be great" had a ring of truth. It didn't matter that the comedy nerd in me was expecting a comedy-romance scene more like something out of Marvellous Mrs Maisel, because that wasn't the show that Phoebe Waller-Bridge was interested in making. There are enough comedy shows for everybody, Dave. If you don't like what you see you can always switch off.

The difference that we're looking at, the difference between what you think you want to write and what you're expected to write, is the difference between a show with jokes and a show that's funny. If you're writing a script with jokes, it's relatively straightforward to see the aim of the comedy, even if it doesn't work. It's that musical rhythm again – set-up joke, set-up joke – that gets you in the habit of knowing when to laugh.

And anyway, Fleabag did have comedy. Miranda was not the first comic to directly address the camera (according to Barry Cryer, that honour belongs to Arthur Askey), but Fleabag ran with the notion and took it to places we hadn't seen since Michael Caine did similar from a male point of view in Alfie. A lot of Fleabag is very funny, check out the pilot which has plenty of proper jokes (and a few more lines in the Obama scene than I had given credit for).

In recent years I've met more new writers who have funny ideas but haven't yet learned properly how to write jokes. They continue to resist learning precisely because of this aversion to the seeming artificiality of the rhythm.

What if the script you're writing is a comedy-drama? (Which is what commissioners constantly telling us they're looking for). What if you're trying to deal with a very serious subject? Do you crowbar in jokes for the sake of it?

My argument has always been that it's still possible to write about dark subject matter and have jokes. What could be darker than a sitcom about bomb disposal units in Afghanistan? Yet Bluestone 42 was a consistently laugh-out-loud show. However dark a situation may be, comedy will always find a way in.

As with everything about comedy scripts, it all comes back to character. If you can create a character as compelling as Fleabag then you can take them wherever you want – dark, light or whimsically amusing, the choice is yours. Is there something original about your character, even if they are familiar? What do they want? And what do they get? And is their failure to get what they want a result of a flaw in their character meaning they're trying to get something they can't have?

I want jokes. But if you can show me funny, I'll take that for now.

SUMMARY

We're happy to enjoy the rhythm of jokes punctuated by laughter, but only when there's an audience in the room. We've lost the habit of watching narrative comedy with that background.

It's possible to have funny stories with fewer jokes.

For these to work, you need a compelling, deeply flawed character.

And I still want jokes. But that's my opinion.

24

View Us a Joke

One of my favourite jobs of the last few years was writing for Lee Mack's sitcom Not Going Out. Lee wrote nearly all the episodes with Daniel Peak, but for six series I was one of a small team coming up with extra ideas and jokes.

I was very excited when the first episode I'd worked on was due to air. I knew the show was popular on comedy forums, and vanity dictated I would have to investigate the day after the show went out. Perhaps someone would point out one of my jokes as an example of the show's brilliance.

I was right about the positive responses, but there was no mention of my, or indeed anyone's jokes. A lot of hours went into the writing and funnying-up of that script, but there was only one moment that everyone kept going on about. Lee and his best mate Tim (Tim Vine) were in a kids' toy shop. There was a short montage over music of Lee and Tim holding up silly toys and pulling funny faces. Then Tim walked into a plastic ball pond and fell over.

I can't describe the many different ways the forum users found to describe the hilarity of that moment. I was too busy being annoyed that no one had appreciated our fabulous verbal dexterity and punnery. Who would have guessed that the biggest laugh in the script would have come from the stage direction "TIM WALKS INTO BALL POND. HE FALLS OVER"?

If you think you know what kind of humour you like, you're almost certainly wrong.

Although we mostly refuse to admit it, we are a nation of slapstick lovers. A universe. Nothing makes the whole world laugh more than Denis Norden's momentary removal of sympathy, when a man falls over.

I'm indebted to Pauline McGowan and the market research team at The Nursery who recently carried out a thorough examination of what makes audiences laugh. Around half the people interviewed identified themselves as witty, but less than half of them were described as such by their friends.

And in a neat reversal of these figures, less than 20 per cent of those interviewed identified slapstick as their favourite form of comedy, but on the basis of quite detailed research it was worked out that for almost half those interviewed, slapstick was the comedy they loved most. Next time you pat yourself on the back for having such a sophisticated sense of humour, watch a clip of Tim Vine falling over in a plastic ball pond.

It makes sense if you think about it. Thousands of people go to comedy clubs up and down the country every week, but the comedians who consistently sell out the huge venues for weeks at a time are Lee Evans and Michael McIntyre. McIntyre is not a man who revels in wordplay, he and Evans are hugely popular because they pull funny faces and cause audience members to literally clutch their sides with laughter.

Benny Hill was one of the most popular comedians in the world. He performed loads of visual gags, many lifted directly from Marx Brothers movies, that were popular partly because they featured attractive women in their underwear, but mainly because he was always falling over.

Jokes involve words, and a level of engagement and sophistication to understand the intricate nuance of language, principally English. Not everyone speaks English, and fewer of them will understand word play. But everyone in the world gets it when that man falls over.

Writers who come through the ranks of radio comedy, me included, don't always remember how important it is that TV and movie are visual media.

I'm not a fan of Mrs Brown's Boys, but it's easy to see why that show is so popular. Man dressed as a lady falling over is one of the oldest gags in the book, but years of performing the show live, plus a deconstructive approach to the artificiality of the TV studio make for a winning combination.

It's hugely popular, as was another recent BBC audience sitcom Miranda, which also scored heavily on the visual gag hit rate. People still go to live theatre but in its most popular form we have panto, which as Jeffrey Richards points out in his book The Golden Age of Pantomime, is a form that combined the classic mimes of the Italian comedia dell'arte that pre-dates Shakespeare, 19th century burlesque and Greek satire.

Yes, satire. For centuries "fat man" was shorthand for "greedy, rich bloke", and the sight of him lying flat on his arse during the matinee run of Jack and the Beanstalk achieved a more powerful message than half-a-dozen of the finest well-crafted gags on Have I Got News for You.

We're back with "Show don't tell." When you're writing the words of a spoken joke, it's funnier if you can paint a visual picture rather than having to spell out your meaning. In silent comedy, with no words to help, you are forced to rely entirely on "show".

With so much comedy on TV and at the movies, it's easy to forget that in most cases it works best when you're in the room with it. Not just because going to see a live show is always more exciting than seeing it on the telly, but also because anything can happen. We sometimes forget that comedy is the great democratic art form. If the audience aren't laughing at your comedy drama, it's not the end of the world. if they're not laughing at your comedy comedy, it is.

Mrs Brown's Boys makes millions of people laugh their heads off, and it keeps comedy alive. I've learned to accept that you liking Mrs Brown doesn't make you a bad person. You're wrong, of course, but then so am I.

What's the best way to bring visual humour to your scripts?

Like everything else, it is, as ever, about character.

Mr Bean may be a sketchily drawn idiot savant but everything he does is in persona. David Hyde Pierce brings incredible subtlety to his performance as Niles Crane, but every pernickety little move gives insight into who he is, as well as delivering plenty of big, dialogue-free laughs.

The writer and performer Julian Dutton, who wrote the series Pompidou with Matt Lucas, is one of our leading experts on silent comedy. There's not much Julian doesn't know about the genre, and he's written a book called Visual Comedy In The Age Of Sound, which I highly recommend.

If you go to Julian's website he's put up the pilot script he wrote that became Pompidou. It's fascinating to look at a 37-page script without a single word of dialogue.

Julian kindly made a list for me of what he calls The Seven Silent Jokes. They read a little like definitions of verbal jokes, but instead of hearing the words you're seeing them. He starts with **repetition.** A great example I can think of is Sideshow Bob in The Simpsons. We all know the animation cliché of people standing on the prongs of a rake and it jumping up to whack them in the face. Bob is in a garden with a whole bunch of rakes, and he stands on each one. There are about ten "Ouch!"es in ten seconds. You know he's going to do it. It's still funny.

The second is **sudden appearances or disappearances.** Delboy falling through the bar is an obvious example.

Then there's **separate realities**, which feels similar to the verbal "reversal" or "surprise" gag. You look at one thing, and it turns into something else. Some of the greatest comedians, including Steve Martin and Tommy Cooper, were also magicians.

There's another lovely moment in The Simpsons when Homer buys a barbecue kit: it looks beautiful in the garden, but what we've been looking at is the box it came in, and as that is moved away we see Homer's attempt at building it: a pile of mess in his garden of bricks, charcoal and burnt rubble.

Humans behaving like non-human things is another category, and always good for a laugh. I remember an advert from years back about dog owners who look like their dogs. They didn't just look like them, they acted like them. Reverse that and you have the gorilla playing the drums on In The Air Tonight.

Objects behaving like other objects is another example, there's a nice one in the Pompidou pilot of a Sikh motorcyclist. He gets off his bike and takes off his turban, which is actually a motorbike helmet, he has his real turban underneath. Our first sighting of Leslie Nielsen, playing a doctor in Airplane!, is of him listening to his in-flight radio with a stethoscope for earphones.

In another moment in Pompidou, illustrating what Julian calls **a collision of ideas**, a woman is walking through a department store holding a plant. As she walks through the cosmetics section, someone sprays her wrist with perfume, then she walks through the garden section and someone sprays her plant with fly spray.

Finally Julian mentions **misunderstandings**. There's a lovely part in one of Buster Keaton's movies where he is running away from the scene of a crime and bumps into a policeman, and manages to convince the policeman he's not running but dancing like a busker for money.

Watch Edgar Wright's movies. He's always looking for new ways to tell familiar stories. Objects appear in frame in funny ways, people leave in funny ways, music is used for comic effect. You can do all of this, and if you're lucky enough to get your script made, actors will love you for giving them funny things to do without having to speak.

Keep crafting the lovely conversational gags, but don't forget the number one rule of comedy: if in doubt, make a man fall over.

SUMMARY

Spoken jokes are popular throughout the English-speaking world. Visual jokes are enjoyed across the entire planet.

Remember that most jokes are "a momentary removal of sympathy." Nothing defines that quite like the sight of a man falling over.

There are seven types of visual jokes – repetition, sudden appearances or disappearances, separate realities, humans behaving like non-human things, objects behaving like other objects, a collision of ideas and misunderstandings.

But like all jokes, spoken or seen, the best ones are always character-based.

25

What Are You Laughing At?

There's a famous quote about analysing comedy, likening it to dissecting a frog: "Nobody laughs, and the frog dies." Which is funny, thereby proving the only rule of comedy, which is that there are no rules in comedy.

The joke, first made by EB White, is often attributed to Barry Cryer. Indeed, he was the first person I heard that quote from. Anyone who ever spent time in the company of Barry knew that he never told a joke he didn't write without attributing it, and sure enough he preceded it by saying the observation was made by EB White.

Does that matter? It matters to joke writers, who understandably get angry when people steal their jokes and pass them off as their own, but for those not steeped in comedy analysis – in other words, the vast majority of the human race – attributing the line to Barry is a useful indicator to them that it's probably going to be funny.

Well, that's my analysis of it. Like many comedy anoraks I love nothing more than to dissect humour like a frog-botherer in a lab coat, take apart every scene, character trait and joke and work out what's right – or wrong. I am not a fun person to watch comedy on TV with. And with dead frogs in science labs in my head I've been wary of inflicting this nerdiness on a wider public.

I feel I've been given permission by another stand-up comic, Simon Evans, who argues eloquently that analysing jokes is a worthwhile occupation. "It's one of the great myths that if you analyse humour, it dies," he said. "If the joke has strong genes, it will come through." On Twitter, top comic Gary Delaney shows the workings of gags he no longer uses.

Broadly speaking, most jokes involve an element of surprise. If you know what's coming, you won't laugh. Except when you do know like when, after another disgusted woman has walked away from Sanjeev Bhaskar's embarrassing dating character in "Goodness Gracious Me", he says "Check please". Or when Dafydd Thomas gets to the point in the sketch where he will say "I am the only gay in the village".

Another rule of comedy broken, laughing at something that is the opposite of a surprise. Closely related to that is the comedy of recognition. Everybody knows that you buy stuff that you don't often use but it took a five-minute routine by Jerry Seinfeld to interpret it for you in a new way.

As an exercise, I went on Twitter and picked out a random selection of gags from some of my favourite funny people. I've gone for the written gags, although visual humour on Twitter is becoming increasingly sophisticated.

Karl Sharro (@KarlRemarks) is one of the funniest people on Twitter. A Lebanese architect living in London, he has a unique take on middle Eastern affairs, and the western attitude to Arabs. Here are some of his jokes.

In these difficult times, I have to pretend I'm not an Arab. I will try not to introduce algebra to the west or translate Greek philosophy.

This is a joke that could come across as po-faced if delivered by a well-meaning westerner. Karl's ability to make this joke about himself gives him a set-up that contains a truth that speaks for millions across the world. The punchline is both a celebration of positive Arab role models and a great piece of self-deprecation.

I like the way this next joke takes an occasionally mentioned fact (the US is a nation of immigrants) and uses Trump's narrative on himself. It's quite rare for a topical joke to achieve the aims of satire but I think this one comes close:

Send those fundamentalist illegal immigrants to the US back where they came from. 17th century Europe.

Applying Aristotle's Three-Act structure to this, in Act One, Karl uses a version of a phrase – "send them back" – that we recognise instantly as a racist statement. But this is Karl, so we know to expect a subversion of that proclamation. The first sentence is therefore also the inciting incident and the complications in Act Two. How can he be saying that? The twist is, he's not talking about modern day Arabs, the punchline is that he means the British and Dutch religious extremists who first colonised the country.

Jokes, like sketches, and most movies and novels, begin in a familiar place. "A man walks into a bar." Course he does. Then something odd happens, that's a twist that'll take us to the punchline.

Summer Ray's jokes start in a normal place, and you think they stay there. It takes a moment to realise she's led you somewhere completely different. Like this:

I'm still not entirely clear on what The Spice Girls want.

Brevity is indeed the soul of wit, as Shakespeare expressed it most eloquently in one of his myriad plays, the particular name escapes me, can't quite remember which but it will almost certainly have been one of the comedies, I should probably have looked it up but have chosen instead to contradict the opening phrase of this sentence for the purposes of comedy. Summer Ray however is brilliant at creating short jokes, beautifully crafted and self-contained. Like this seven-word gem:

Sometimes I contradict myself all the time.

Once again, a joke that has the rhythm of music.

Paul B Davies, aka @thewritertype, has been writing great jokes for more than 40 years. When I was starting out he mentored me and taught me many of the skills of joke writing, by his own examples. In my teenage years I thought he was one of the most original writers I'd met. Four decades on I haven't changed that view. Here's one:

Someday we'll look back on this and laugh, betraying our position to the roaming vigilantes, who'll drag us from our cave and execute us.

That's a joke from someone who has thought a lot about our world. It starts with a familiar phrase, immediately followed by a joke that directly contradicts that opening line. Normally we look back and laugh when things are okay, but things are currently so bad that we're still at the mercy of roaming vigilantes. That on its own is pretty funny, but the final section takes the gag from the second part to its extreme conclusion. A joke that manages to be funny, scary, and evocative of a dystopian future in 24 words.

Even if he wasn't creating jokes, Paul would be a brilliant writer. He has achieved success across the entire range of writing – sketches, plays, movies, and now he's a novelist, praised by Stephen King no less. His command of vocabulary and attention to detail ensure that every sentence is rich with meaning and atmosphere.

Confuse future archaeologists by burying your pets in elaborate military uniforms.

Paul has achieved a lot of success as a radio writer, and this joke helps indicate why. It conjures up a very funny visual image, a dog dressed up as an army general, but as ever with Paul takes the joke to another level by painting a second picture. We can imagine the look on the archaeologist's face, 300 years from now as they discover Fido in a grey-buttoned suit with medals and epaulettes.

You could argue that "Confuse future archaeologists" is not a familiar place to start. I would disagree because the form of the joke, based on the famous Viz magazine "Top Tips", has itself become so familiar that we are not mystified because of the way the joke is phrased.

Incidentally Paul is a talented cartoonist, as is @MooseAllain, whose jokes also create great pictures.

Moose specialises in word play, and frequently comes up with brilliant puns. You may feel that there are too many puns on Twitter already, and you may be right, but Moose's puns always feel fresh, and veer away from the obvious. For example:

I've never been on the London Eye. I don't move in the right circles.

As with Paul, the pleasure is enhanced by a strong visual element.

Whenever I buy wine gums I get the shopkeeper to let me taste one, then if it's ok I buy the whole packet.

I love the silliness of that line, you couldn't even call it a pun as we're being asked to equate wine with wine gums. I must have heard people joke hundreds of times about wine gums making you drunk, but once again Moose goes past the obvious gag and finds a new and satisfying variation.

I hope I haven't ruined these jokes for you by analysing them. They're still funny, and if you're not following these people on Twitter already then do so now, and I guarantee there'll be more.

SUMMARY

Analysing jokes will help you understand why some work and others don't.

Taking one lesson from each of these master craftspeople I would say:

One of the greatest sources of unique material is you (Karl).

Keep it simple (SummerRay).

Read more, understand the world (Paul).

Look beyond the obvious jokes (Moose).

26

Get Them While They're Young

Once upon a time there was a TV Channel called BBC and it showed everything! Children's stories at lunchtime, old films in the afternoon, news in the evening and plays and comedy at night. At ten o'clock the Channel would close down, say "night night" and come back next day.

Nowadays if you want to write for children there are more channels than there are hours in the day to watch them. Most children like big funny programmes and companies that make them order batches in industrial quantities.

Where else, apart from radio, is it possible to explore such a huge range of subjects and in such varied styles across so many platforms? Have a look at the CBBC website and marvel at the spread of content from interactive video games to silly quizzes and random joke generators.

If you want to develop a career as a comedy writer in the UK, you need to think of writing for kids not as a stepping-stone to the future, but as a project you want to be involved with for its own sake.

And why wouldn't you? If you want to write for mainstream TV and you're not interested in soaps, crime or hospitals, you've already opted out of 90% of the opportunities that are already out there.

Apart from not using rude words, and where possible avoiding booze, sex and gambling, writing for kids is more or less the same as writing for adults.

Like all TV, Children's was already witnessing a massive upheaval before the pandemic, and this has accelerated. Streaming was changing our viewing habits. Audiences watching shows when they first appear on TV have been declining for years.

As far back as 2015 we were visited on a Horrible Histories writing day by a CBBC executive, to warn us that YouTube was taking over, and children would never again watch anything lasting longer than two minutes. And that was years before Tik Tok.

Video on demand, streaming, subscription TV, whatever you call it, it's growing exponentially. Once the shiny glamour and novelty of Disney Plus and Amazon Prime wears off, having quality content remains the ultimate priority for all commissioners.

That means, hopefully, the quality content you make. And that's the most important point.

Channels always need content.

This isn't about reinventing the wheel. The biggest hit shows aren't necessarily the most original. Horrible Histories took an already massively successful book series and the sensibility of Blackadder to create a truly innovative show. Start with the familiar and add something special. The same rules as apply across all creative endeavour.

What are the most popular shows on Children's TV? You might be surprised to discover the answers. For three to six-year-olds it's Paw Patrol. And the favourite show of seven to 12-year-olds, which I would never have guessed in a thousand years is... The Simpsons.

You must reach number five before you find a BBC show in either chart – Bing for the six and unders, and (hooray!) Horrible Histories for the older group.

Shows that are more popular with kids than these include Peppa Pig, Scooby Doo – yikes! – Spongebob Squarepants and Britain's Got Talent.

Britain's Got Talent! Here I am trying to offer words of encouragement about the prospect of your show being made, or even a chance for you to write in the field. Meanwhile the most popular programmes have either already been written, in a different country, or they're not even asking for you unless you can script an act with a novelty juggler or a power ballad crooner.

If you want to write for CBeebies or CBBC, you should watch what's on there at the moment.

Let me sum up each channel in two words:

CBeebies: Justin Fletcher. CBBC: Tracy Beaker.

If you have small children or have for whatever reason found yourself blinking at the garishly bright colours, cartoon animals and sing-song narrators of toddler TV, you will at some point have seen Justin, aka Mr Tumble.

Justin is the heart and soul of CBeebies, he represents almost everything the channel stands for. He's funny, anarchic, inspirational, and as inclusive as it is ever possible for a middle-aged white male to be. Once you accept that, almost everything else fits into place.

I don't know how many hundreds of shows Justin has made over the last decade but check your schedules and there's bound to be at least one on every day. If you want to get a feel for how to write for CBeebies, consider watching 20 minutes of Justin every day as your introduction.

For CBBC I nearly chose the novelist Jacqui Wilson, but her creation Tracy Beaker also brings you the actor Dani Harmer, who played Tracy and whose shows Dani's House and Dani's Castle sated the appetite of Beaker fans, while waiting for Wilson's next TV adaptation The Dumping Ground to bed in. 200 episodes later it remains hugely popular and has for years been the show where new writers have learned their craft.

Many CBBC shows are adapted from kids' books. Are you an avid reader of fiction? Can you find an original way of turning your favourite ultra-obscure volume into something televisual? (By the way The Famous Five and Harry Potter are not obscure.)

The Next Step and Almost Never are aspirational comedy dramas about making it in the world of entertainment. Danger Mouse and Dennis the Menace are the current animation favourites. Danny and Mick are the slapstick heirs to the Chuckle Brothers, and the CBBC bosses love them, so you should too.

If you're looking to write for CBeebies you probably know the score – bright colours, animals, simple stories and learning to navigate social relationships. You can understand why Peppa Pig is so popular – those porcine pals often argue with each other and let's face it, why should we expect a pig to get on with a rabbit? Although I wonder if that sort of inter-species bickering might be less tolerated by the educationally leaning BBC.

You might want to check out Andy and The Band – Andy is Andy Day, who for years has been the John Noakes of CBeebies. Going on safari, deep sea diving, playing with dinosaurs. His first attempt at comedy drama is proving a big hit not just with the toddlers, but the all-important transitional five to eight years-old age group. Tomorrow's CBBC watchers, in other words.

Without trying to second guess your own writing desires, it's worth being aware of how the execs are thinking. I heard a phrase "Bringing the UK to the world and the world to the UK" which sounds a little bit weird and potentially dodgy but I think I get the sentiment. The BBC is probably one of the last remaining British icons respected across the world and Children's TV want to remain a part of that.

The other phrase you hear a lot is "We need to grow the audience with us, go to where they are." Which I think translates as "grab them when they're toddlers, hold on to them as they get older, then keep them by getting our content on all their platforms for viewing,"

The good news is, Children's' TV wants all the stuff we keep begging the other TV channels to make more of – sketch shows, animation, narrative comedy.

At this stage in your writing career, this may seem like a list of asks to get very excited about. On the other hand, it's almost as though there are too many things on offer, and if you're already squeezing comedy development and writing into a busy life and work schedule, you need to focus on one or two things and concentrate on where your strengths lie.

You might not necessarily know what those strengths are until you start exploring them in more detail. If we're all going to live happily ever after, we may need some expert guidance.

Happily, expert guidance is at hand.

SUMMARY

If you want to write for TV, Children's is a good place to start.

Writing for children isn't so different to writing for adults.

Every children's channel has an identity. Have a look around them and think about how you might contribute.

27
Writing You Could Have Gotten Away with If It Hadn't Been for Those Pesky Kids

I said in the last chapter that there are few differences between writing for kids and for grown-ups.

There are other constraints and opportunities beyond my knowledge and skill set. I spoke to several people about what these might be.

George Poles is a lovely man and a very funny writer, what's more relevant here is that he has worked for many years as a script editor on loads of kids' TV shows including Dani's House, Chucklevision and multi-award-winning Hank Zipzer.

George reads dozens of scripts every year for kids' narrative shows and has kindly agreed to share his top tips for writers working on ideas for scripts, or scripts for shows being made.

Thanks George!

"Here you are, my nine tips for writing for kids...

1) The international audience is ever more important. Lots of your viewers may be working in their second language or watching dubbed versions that have been translated overly-literally. Be careful about your use of idiom - not all your audience may get it. If I may be allowed to misquote Guardians of the Galaxy...Rocket: His people are completely literal. Idioms are gonna go right over his head. Drax: Nothing goes over my head. My reflexes are too fast. I'd catch it.

This goes for what seem like common joke structures too. On a show I worked on recently, several writers tried to use the "He's about as useful as a [chocolate teapot/glass hammer/ejector seat in a helicopter] type of gag and none of the US, French, German or Brazilian broadcast partners understood them at all.

2) Relatedly, make sure your scripts are inclusive and reflect

diversity. (Dave adds: This is especially true in the US, where diversity is built into every pitch for the streaming giants.)

3) Kids quite properly have restrictions on their acting hours, so it's important for adult cast members to share the load. It's often useful to have some scenes in your script with adults only.

4) If your series has a title character, make sure that character is always active and has plenty of the best lines. They're the character the executive producer and broadcasters fell in love with. Beware of spending too much time focusing on the fun sidekick.

5) Every series will have at least one script that doesn't go right. For whatever reason it won't gel with the production company or broadcast partners. It ends up going through a bunch of major drafts or complete rewrites. If it happens to be your script, do your best not to let it get you down - it's not you, it's them. (Note from Dave – wish I'd known that when I was working on a long-running TV series and my script was completely rewritten but there you go).

6) Again, don't feel bad if you sit down to watch your episode only to find it bears worryingly little resemblance to your script. Lots of things can happen during production that force major re-writes.

7) If you're asked for a bunch of episode pitches, the makeweight, quarter-thought-through idea you bunged in at the last minute to fill out the page will be the one that gets picked. Don't pitch something you don't want to write.

8) Genius is great but ultimately less likely to get you hired for a second series than turning in drafts on time, to the right length, and not being an arse.

9) Every script is a calling card. Some of the people reading them today will be industry leaders tomorrow. Do your best to make them remember you for the right reasons."

Thanks George. Once again, almost every note above applies to whatever you're writing for every age.

Jeremy Salsby has made bucket loads of successful kids' TV shows including Sorry I've Got No Head, Friday Download and the current hit comedy drama Almost Never.

"When we pitched Almost Never," he said, "we wrote two scripts and a pitch deck which was an overview of the series, an outline for future series and a character breakdown. A lot then changed between pitch and first transmission, as it always does."

It's important for writers to bring their own style and sensibility to the show. Jeremy asks for very short story pitches – "A" plots mainly - to see if the writer 'gets' the show.

"In terms of writer's brief I ask to meet with each potential new writer. We discuss the show, which I ask them to watch so I can get a feel for their views on episodes, characters, stories, tone, drama, comedy, strengths, weaknesses and so on. A story pitch ALWAYS tells me if I think they're right for the show. Then once commissioned we go to beats - and spend a long time on that, then go to script."

Like everyone else I've spoken to about this, Jeremy doesn't distinguish between the work he does for adult TV and radio, and for children's.

"'Writing for kids' is a phrase I've never used in any of the shows I've made for CBBC. It's a comedy or a drama or a sketch show."

One difference revolves around the quantities of show made for Childrens', compared to other channels. CBBC commission in American-sized chunks of 13 or 20 episodes in a series. A common requirement in the US is for you to create a "bible". This is a manual that tells you and your producers everything we need to know about the show.

Jeremy says "The bible should come at the end of the first series because that's when you know what the show is." But if you're looking to create many episodes of a long-running show, I'd advise you to consider creating one. Type "TV show bible examples" into your search engine of choice and you'll find plenty of inspiration.

One that caught my attention was Steven Moffat's original pitch for Press Gang. Bear in mind this is right at the start of his career, no one had any idea who he was.

This is the opening paragraph:

PRESS GANG

"Take a town called Norbridge, ill at ease with the recent mixing of its rural tradition and new industry now already in decline; a town that had eagerly spread itself with new estates and new people to embrace a new prosperity that has never come; a place of youthful discontent and unrest."

What strikes me about this is I could have told you that it was the original pitch for a dark Netflix comedy drama in the vein of Orange Is the New Black or Stranger Things, and you wouldn't have had a reason to doubt me.

Recently I was working with a couple of writers on their latest sitcom script. I wondered if there might be a way of coming up with a slightly different pitch and offering it to CBBC.

The thought hadn't crossed their minds but as soon as I said it I could see them getting excited at the prospect.

What are you working on now? Is it a dark comedy for Channel Four? A family sitcom for BBC One? A young comedy drama for BBC Three? Look closer at what you're writing.

How much would you have to change to pitch to CBBC?

I bet you'll be surprised.

SUMMARY

If you want to write for children, be aware that you're often pitching to international markets.

Concentrate on the main character, not the sidekick. Wise advice whatever you're working on.

Can you look at the current project you're working on and find a way to pitch it as a kids' TV show? Chances are you can.

28

Humans – Who Needs 'Em?

I've just looked up at the sky, there's a grand piano about to drop on my head so I'd better run out of the way and start discussing animati- too late.

The most popular programmes for kids in the UK, you know now, include PAW Patrol and Peppa Pig for the six-and-unders, and The Simpsons and Scooby Doo for the seven to 12 age bracket.

What single word could possibly link these four series? Yes, if you want eyeballs for the shows you write then you need to write a few that pop out of their sockets on stalks.

I promise no more tortuous attempts to explore the world of animation using cartoon metaphors. That's all folks. DAVE STOP NOW.

Pretty much from its first movie appearance and before Walt Disney was born, animation was synonymous with comedy. Early pioneers like Emile Cohl and George Mélies used trickery and magic for comic effect. Disney's gently amusing talking mice were quickly matched by Warner Brothers' smart-ass, sarcastic wise-cracking wabbit. These two tropes have more or less defined the world of animation ever since.

Loveable Mickey Mouse and snarky Bugs Bunny. As Cheers writer Rob Long has pointed out, comedy writers always prefer coming up with lines for Bugs. And nothing made me laugh more in my own childhood than seeing Wile E. Coyote run over by a bus or blown up by his own Acme dynamite sticks.

The tone of surrealism has been cranked up by more recent shows like Gumball and Adventure Time. But in the same way that writing for kids is no different to writing for adults, writing animation is pretty much the same as writing for any other forms – apart from a few ways which I'll come to in a minute.

CBBC are desperate for new animation. The Children's Animation Scheme is developing ideas from lesser-known animators. "We want and need more of it," says Sarah Muller, the head at time of writing of the channel. Children's and Education Director Patricia Hidalgo has long talked of the BBC searching for "a child-friendly UK equivalent of The Simpsons."

The BBC Commissioners say they're looking for "Fast paced character-driven comedy" and "Sharply written family sitcom." Sarah Muller has said "There's no reason why this should be the sole province of US studios. You can have a more complex narrative style. A diverse family set up. Widen up characters and locations. You can take risks."

Character-driven comedy, family sitcom, it's the same requirements however weird and surreal you decide to go. What makes animation different?

"wwwwWWWWHHUUUU!?" Pendleton Ward's original pitch document begins, then continues "Adventure Time is about two close friends: Jake, a wise old dog with a big kind heart, and Finn, a silly kid who wants more than anything else to become a great hero." Nothing there offers the vaguest hint of what's to come. Apart from that "wwwwWWWWHHUUUU!?" at the start.

Have a look at some of the early episodes of the Danger Mouse reboot.

A typical episode begins in the centre of London – black cabs, red buses, commuters. Moments later a stampede of angry rainbow ponies sends cars and pedestrians flying.

Danger Mouse and Penfold come to the rescue. "It's a bit early for all this, isn't it, Chief?" Penfold says, "I haven't even had my porridge."

"Evil doesn't have a snooze button, Penfold!"

A mouse spy vaulting over cars, and a stampede of angry

rainbow ponies – that's how animation differs from writing for real people. But character wise Danger Mouse is still a rodent James Bond, and Penfold his hapless side kick.

Ben Ward, who probably knows more about how to write comedy for kid's TV than anyone in the entire universe, sums up what he's looking for with every Danger Mouse script:

"Strong character. Big story. Funny hat. Character will always give you the answer."

"Kid's TV looks wacky and zany, and people think it's anarchic," he says, "but if you want to write for it you have to start thinking about precision."

Animation lets children go to places that live action can't.

"Things can happen to characters that don't happen in the real world, without scary real-world consequences. This makes it fertile ground for the comedy writer as the action can be extreme."

But as anyone involved with animation will tell you, it's not the animation that makes for a successful TV series, it's the characters. The animators, like actors, get inspiration from characters. The script is their blueprint. You still have to work hard to give characters flaws, inner lives and outer conflicts, moral conflicts. This is what makes kids come back for more.

Paw Patrol is quite sophisticated as a work of three-dimensional animation. But The Simpsons, Peppa Pig, Scooby Doo – I mean, they're barely two-dimensional. This is what matters above all else: make sure your character is three-dimensional, worry about the physical form they take after.

SUMMARY

Writing animation is not much different to writing for humans.

Action can be more extreme. Weird things can happen. But

characters still require believability. Think Bugs Bunny. Danger Mouse. Gnasher the dog.

As Ben Ward says: Strong character. Big story. Funny hat.

29

Stand Up for Your Writes

It feels strange to use a word like "writing" when discussing stand-up comedy. Such is the conversational nature of stand-up, half the audience think you're making it up as you go along, and even if the audience are reduced to tears by your sharp observations, they'll struggle afterwards to recall a word. "I saw a brilliant stand-up last night." Really, what was their name? "I can't remember. She had red hair." What jokes? "I can't remember. Oh yeah, she had this hilarious bit about dogs. Actually it might have been cats. Actually that was the bloke before her..."

It's almost as if the material is, well, immaterial. New acts already start out quite professional compared to when my shambolic contemporaries emerged. They look good, engage with the audience, and carry themselves confidently, having successfully studied the greats and the mediocre who fill endless hours of space on TV, YouTube and TikTok.

The one thing they can't fake is a point of view. Just as it can take a writer years to find their voice, so a stand-up will have to perform a lot of gigs before finding the persona on stage that they are comfortable with.

This isn't always the case. The first time I saw Stewart Lee was in 1989 in Edinburgh when he was a student, trying out material in the venue where I was doing my show. I don't remember any of the lines, but was immediately taken with the person on stage – and I don't think I've ever seen him look or sound any different in the intervening decades. Others I remember arriving fully formed from day one were Jo Brand, Jeremy Hardy, Lee Evans and Harry Hill.

They were the exceptions. Paul Merton, Eddie Izzard and Jack Dee were among many who were perfectly good when they began but took a while to stand out from the crowd.

The best stand-ups find laughs in many ways. A comic's

physical appearance, the way they move, or stand still, can be as important as what they say. Facial expressions, used well and sparingly, will enhance the set. Comedians working regularly, repeating their lines four or five times a week, may suddenly work out a way of saying the same line that will bring a much bigger laugh, or a response to a heckle may end up being incorporated into the routine.

But with very few exceptions (Jerry Sadowitz the only one I remember from my generation), comics do write their material down. Even if you aren't hearing many words, there's a large written element behind even the most visual of routines. And in the same way that the best jokes in any script or story are true to the character, the strongest stand-up material personifies the character we're watching on stage.

If you're a comedian and don't think writing is important you should start working with someone who just writes. If you think comedians don't need to be writers then you aren't paying attention to your job.

Over the years I've seen Michael McIntyre called all kinds of name, especially unflattering ones by his fellow comics. One word I've never seen used though is "writer". On the surface McIntyre's routines are viewed as the elongating of a single reasonably familiar observation into three minutes of visual buffoonery, sold to the undiscerning punters through a mixture of grinning tics and boundless high energy.

There's some truth to this, but look closely, and you'll see how much work has gone into those routines. Watch the clip on YouTube where he talks about travelling on public transport: there's probably nothing in those three minutes that hasn't crossed most comedic minds. However, as the old fella used to say, it's the way he tells them.

The routine starts with a few funny mimes and two nice jokes. First, the observation that everyone reads the same paper on the London Underground, so why can't one person read it out to the whole of the carriage? Followed by a lovely left-field remark about how turning the page of an old broadsheet newspaper was like folding a tablecloth.

Two big laughs and we're only half a minute in. Both are comic embellishments to a familiar setting that I don't remember seeing before. And I have a great memory for other people's jokes.

They serve merely as a set-up to the bigger story on the train. This is where McIntyre scores above many of his rivals. He is a proper storyteller who understands the narrative power of a comedy routine. Taken as a whole, McIntyre's two and three minute routines are like Aristotle's Three Act stories. They start in normality and build towards a climax, with big laughs along the way.

Today, we're told in the tube story, Act One, that the train is full. It's the fullest he's ever seen it, and there are a few visual laughs on the way to the inciting incident that sends us into the heart of the story. Which is, a man is going to try and cram himself onto an already full train. Act Two. The laughs are coming regularly now, as McIntyre describes the complications that arise from this twist. Having failed to get on the train, the man walks away. Is that the end? Of course not, he hasn't given up, he's giving himself a run-up.

Like all the best writers, McIntyre has escalated the tension as the story unfolds. The man gets his body in, but the head is sticking out. The words are sparse in this routine, but McIntyre is painting a vivid picture. The doors hit the man's head – "No one needs to get on this badly, get out man get out!" And they hit his head again. How will this man get in? Will he get in? Is it all lost for the man? We want to know. Act Three gives us the resolution. The man moves slightly to one side, and uses the force of the tube door to knock his head into the train.

There follows a short explanation – "He's in!" and a little punchline recalling a gag from earlier in the routine. Three minutes of big laughs. Watch the clip, and you may feel it's very slight, three minutes of nothing. But think about how even the most prolific stand-ups rarely create more than an hour of material in a year – and you're looking at slightly less than three weeks' work.

A lot of those hours will have been spent trying out the lines in small clubs, watching back physical moves and refining them. And while as a piece of writing, the routine would struggle to fill a page, even using double spacing and a big font size, the work that went into it will have been as painstaking as anything you may have seen on TV: a key scene in a funny sitcom, a stand-out sketch on a popular show.

If you want to know how the best comics come up with their material, have a listen to Stuart Goldsmith's Comedian's Comedian podcast, in particular the episodes featuring Gary Delaney and Jimmy Carr.

Every comic has a different way of coming up with material. For James Acaster it's always a work in progress, constantly being improved. One of his recent shows combined making up new characters on stage through improvisation, and writing routines about the minutiae of life for that character.

Hundreds of comics make the annual pilgrimage to Edinburgh, full of optimism and eventually crushed by the daily onslaught of alcohol, successful colleagues and incredible shrinking crowds. Over the weeks, one or two will rise above the rest and be feted by audience and critics.

Who will it be? I've no more idea than anyone else, but those who keep coming back and winning new fans – those will be the comedians who understand that in order to be a consistently successful performer, first you must learn to write.

SUMMARY

Contrary to popular belief, comedians are rarely making it up as they go along.

Ability to write isn't the only element required by a successful comedian, but it's one of the most important.

The best stand-up comedy routines are faithful to that Three Act structure we have been applying to everything throughout the book.

30

A Man Walks into A News Story

In the previous edition of Complete Comedy Writer, I opened this chapter with the following paragraph:

If we're playing percentages, the quickest way to start earning a living writing comedy is probably through coming up with one-line topical jokes.

I think that's still true, and since 2018 the number of opportunities to do this have increased considerably. The paragraph that followed said:

Topical gag writers are among the most sought after professionals in the business. I can think of only about ten people who have kept at it successfully and consistently in the 35 years or so I've been doing this. I did it for about 20 years and even spent a few of those in the Premier Division, but in football terms I was not so much Manchester City as West Ham.

Which is also true.

The problem is, four years after I wrote that paragraph, it's still the same 10 people picking up all the well-paid work writing topical comedy. A few more have come through. The big difference is that many more writers are achieving initial success, but the next step up – training and nurturing by BBC radio - has been removed.

Tony Roche (Succession, The Thick of It), David Baddiel (Baddiel and Newman, Fantasy Football), Debbie Barham (Rory Bremner Show, Loose Ends, About A Dog) all achieved their first credits writing one-line topical jokes.

This initial success brought their names to the attention of producers, who gave them jobs writing on new shows. They quickly became full-time writers. Hung out in the offices of BBC Radio Comedy and learned their craft, and how to develop their own ideas.

We do still have a BBC Radio Comedy office (now incorporated into BBC Sounds) but there are half as many producers and fewer shows. Decades of cuts, underfunding and bullying have made it almost impossible for the BBC to maintain its role as Trainer-In-Chief of the nation's comedy writers.

That doesn't mean you shouldn't give it a go. Being able to write jokes week in, week out about the news will bring you to the attention of producers and performers, hungry for new material. At the very least it will bring you more work as a joke writer.

I spent many enjoyable hours and years writing for News Quiz, The Treatment, Loose Ends, Dead Ringers, Spitting Image, 11 O'clock Show, Have I Got News for You and others, and picked up a few hints about how to write topical jokes.

As mentioned frequently elsewhere, Aristotle's Poetics is still the most useful volume on how to write – yes, even more than Seven Secrets of Successful Screenwriters ("Number Three: Richard Curtis always writes in a nightcap, by the light of a burning candle").

The topical gag structure is slightly more complex than "every story has a beginning, a middle and an end" but not much more.

One-line gags normally have a set-up – have you ever noticed the number of comedians who begin a gag with the phrase "have you ever noticed"? It probably owes its continued existence to one of the greatest comics ever, the American stand-up George Carlin, who said more than 50 years ago "Have you ever noticed anybody driving slower than you is an idiot, and anyone driving faster is a maniac?"

This is a perfect Three Act joke. The question is a classic Act One set up, the observation "all slow drivers are idiots" something you may have noticed. It's in your normal sphere of believability, but it took a comedian to bring the absurdity of it to your attention.

Look at the word "and" in that joke. We don't look at "and" very often do we? It's not the kind of word we think about when writing anything. Here though it is the inciting incident at the end of Act One, the normal world where everyone who drives slower than you is an idiot. He could have said "but", but he said "and". (Possibly the clumsiest sentence I have ever written.)

"But" takes your brain too quickly to the suggestion of an opposite, "and" disguises the complication that is about to come, which is that we're not just talking about slow drivers, we're talking about fast ones.

And here's the second twist, we're talking about you, even though you were laughing in the set up and Act Two because you thought he was talking about someone else.

Hence the punchline: Act Three – every one of us is a crap driver.

If you want to write topical comedy, you'll be pleased to know that most of the joke has already been written for you. Here's the random story I used in the last edition on a rare slow news day: "A decomposed body has been found in the water near Donald Trump's golf resort." Act One – a dead body. I know, that sounds like an inciting incident rather than the everyday world, but admit it, you've watched dozens of shows and read lots of books that begin, page one scene one, with a dead body. In storyland, if not in our own lives, this is the normal world.

The inciting incident that takes us into Act Two is that the body was found near Donald Trump's golf club. What are the consequences of this? Who is the body? Who committed the crime? I saw a few joke responses on Twitter, most of which were degrees of variation on the idea that Trump did it. But the funniest I think came from the great Twitter gag writer @Pundamentalism – "Police confirm identity of body as Uncle Sam".

That's quite a leap from the story, beyond the obvious route taken by everyone else, and no one else got there. You might come up with a funny punchline quite quickly, but the chances are so will everyone else. If Twitter has achieved one good thing for comedy writers, it's made us work harder to find more and funnier angles.

And that's the first thing you need to do when you think of what you believe to be your own hilarious gag. Type the key words from it into Twitter's search engine. You'll be amazed – and depressed – to find most times that a dozen amateur joke-smiths arrived at the same funny place as you.

If you want your jokes to stand out, you're going to have to work harder to find them.

Be different. Go off on a tangent, find a topic where you hear the same obvious jokes being made and try and look at the story from a completely different angle. Read lots of newspapers. For those of you under 35, a newspaper is a device that holds a bunch of stuff you read, except instead of just switching it on you have to go to a shop and buy a new one every day. And – get this, it's made of paper. I know, it's ridiculous, but you'll be surprised how the physical act of reading a paper can sometimes feel more conducive to coming up with gags than swiping through a screen. Sometimes a sentence jumps out and you come up with an instant punchline.

It's been a while since I worked on a topical comedy show. Maybe it's to do with my age, or the world in general, but I've lost the urge to make jokes about the news. I haven't buried my head in the sand but have discovered that mostly ignoring it has done wonders for my mental health.

However, Dan Sweryt is one of those writers I mentioned at the start who has come through in recent years, and he has plenty of excellent advice about how to write topical comedy.

He's kindly agreed to share this with us. Dan says:

"1 Get some writing partners

This is probably the single most useful advice. A lone writer banging out gags often can't see the funny for the clever. With a writing partner you are (a) editing each other's gags, (b) honing your self-editing and script-editing skills and, perhaps most crucially, motivated as you don't want to let the other one(s) down. This is key in generating loads of solid gags for the show.

2 Listen to the show

Don't try and write for a show if you don't know how the topical gags are delivered. Every show has different ways of delivering their jokes.

3 Write properly

Feedline. Gag. Don't write a topper. Don't put your funniest word or the actual gag anywhere but the end of the line.

4 Write loads, write everything

Between myself and my two writing partners, we put in a minimum of five hours each, every week on a single episode, usually more. Our submission is minimum 15 person-hours of work to fill our quota. Think of *every* angle on a story and try write a gag on it.

Write notes about the stories and where you think the gags might be.

Read everything about the story you're writing about. You know why? Because every line in that story is a potential feedline for a gag and if no-one else is reading the other articles, you're the only one coming up with those gags!

The same topics come up. A lot. Covid. Incompetent Tories. Crumbling public services. You have to pull out more and more gags on the same things. Go into <u>*ridiculous*</u> minuscule detail on it, hone right on it to find more gags. It's exhausting. But someone needs to do it, so why not you?

5 Learn how to edit your own jokes

This is a great skill to pick up. It helps to work with a partner and edit each other's lines. We don't always see what's not working with our own stuff. But looking at someone else's gags will improve your own. If you're not editing down, you're probably not (by definition) coming up with the best stuff.

6 Write to the brief

Every topical show has instructions about things like tone, joke length, topics to focus on or avoid. If you can't follow the basic instructions, the over-worked producers and script editors will learn to ignore you.

7 There are opportunities in 'balance'

All BBC shows make an effort to be balanced. And, like all writers, this will be nigh on impossible to manage whilst writing hilarious gags that really give it to the parties currently in charge!

However, that means there are comparatively few gags received about the 'other' political parties. Write gags about them and you're immediately ahead of other writers who don't write those jokes and it's all down to the unique way the BBC is funded.

8 The news is cyclical

Sometimes it feels that 'there's no chance this gag will <u>ever</u> get used again!', but the news is repetitive. However ridiculous a story, some spin on it will come around again and again (and again!) and allow you to pilfer the old ideas in your gags into shiny new ones.

9 Repeatability

Every joke you write can potentially be rewritten for another avenue: either another topical show, a satirical website or even just a Tweet to try and find your audience. YOU WILL HAVE TO REWRITE IT TO FIT THAT PARTICULAR BRIEF THOUGH! Don't forget that and rewrite accordingly.

10 You get used to writing topical gags

The first few series are hard and exhausting, so you may need to take breaks during a series. By your fourth or fifth series it feels - in a way - easier. I mean, it's not 'easier' to write gags upon gags upon gags, but you start to become more conditioned to writing topical gags for weeks upon end. But that's good - *because that's what it's like to be a topical gag-writer*!

BUT

11 Try and write for every episode of the series.

Keep doing this every week for the whole series. Then repeat for every week of every series.

Persistence is fertile."

SUMMARY

Writing topical jokes is the quickest way to build credits, and to become known to BBC producers.

Topical jokes, like all jokes, like everything, follow the Three Act structure. The difference is that the second act – the complication – has already been written.

Writing topical jokes is a learned discipline. Follow Dan's habits and suggestions above and you'll give yourself a good chance of earning those credits.

31
Woke, Jokes and Blokes

Recently I was asked to go on the radio to talk about political correctness in comedy.

That could have been the opening sentence of any blog or article I've written about comedy in the last 35 years.

Why is this being discussed AGAIN??? Haven't we gone round the houses with this a million times? Haven't we established that there are only two possible responses? To the question "is there too much political correctness in comedy" isn't the answer either: YES, you're not allowed to be rude about certain people anymore, it's only banter, it's just a joke...

...or NO, "political correctness" is a phrase invented by the far right to disguise the fact that they want to keep telling racist and sexist jokes, but it sounds better to attack people who disagree with them than to admit they like telling sexist and racist jokes."

In the modern world where all nationalities sit side by side, women are supposed to be treated as equals, and people with disabilities need respect not mockery, refusing to be cruel for the sake of it when writing comedy is a good place to start. Isn't it?

This latest round of why-oh-why-ing was brought about by the cancellation of Jerry Sadowitz's second show as part of the 2022 Edinburgh Festival, after a number of complaints regarding his first. When I wrote the first edition of this book, the controversy was about Mel Brooks, like Jerry a Jewish comedian, who was referring to the "n" word. We Jews in comedy may not control showbiz, as lizard-loving David Icke would have you believe, but we sure know how to make the headlines.

I've made it clear already that when Mel speaks, I listen. This is the man who changed my life and defined a career for me in comedy not once, but twice. First as a teenager, when I saw The Producers and more than anything in the world it made me want to be a comedian. And second in my 40s, when I saw the musical version on Broadway, which made me want to spend the rest of my working life writing comic songs.

Mel answers the above question with a capital Y-E-S. You're not allowed to be rude about certain people anymore. Blazing Saddles is one of the funniest comic movies ever made, which unashamedly wears its liberal pro-black sentiments like a gold sheriff star. When that movie used the "n" word more than 40 years ago, it was unequivocally to illustrate the awful racism favoured by a certain kind of old white man. These men think the best way to deal with people different to them is stick them behind a wall and hope they go away.

Whether you agree with him or not, Mel is technically correct. You cannot use that word in your script anymore, even if you're damning the person from whose mouth it is emanating. Unless you are a black person writing the script, which raises different issues, and in this area I prefer to be guided by the writer rather than my own prejudices.

I love Mel Brooks, in case you haven't noticed. I don't think I ever laughed so much in a cinema as I did when watching Peter Boyle's monster in Young Frankenstein, singing Putting On The Ritz. That was nearly 50 years ago. Knowing what I have since learned about disability and mental illness, would I find it that funny now? I'm not so sure.

Political correctness moves in cycles. The most popular comedy on TV, by a long way, is Mrs Brown's Boys, which is possibly the least politically correct comedy of the last 40 years. Meanwhile, The Mash Report, the most popular online show ever, was cancelled by the BBC at the height of its success.

The show was criticised because of the left-wing views of the presenter Nish Kumar. Ironically getting rid of it meant the removal of a regular slot for self-proclaimed Conservative comedian Geoff Norcott, a funny guy brought onto the show in the interests of balance. I'm not sure why topical comedy has to be treated with the same rules as the actual news but that's not a discussion for these pages.

The occasional arguments about political correctness, "woke" and cancel culture are a popular media topic that help to confirm and usually polarise people's prejudices. Left-wingers say "cancel culture doesn't exist", right-wingers point to cases like that of Sadowitz. But even GB news, the right-wing cheerleader for this angry discussion, seems to have drawn the line at comedians like Andrew Lawrence and Lee Hurst who would be popular with their demographic, but never appear on their shows.

I don't want to get dragged into this painfully unfunny argument, especially when I'd rather be writing comedy, or writing about it.

What matters as far as this book is concerned is that you need to know the best approach.

What can you write about? How can you write comedy with a controversial viewpoint without having to worry that a producer might respond with "I'm not sure you're allowed to say that anymore"?

From my own view I don't want to give up putting difficult issues into my comedy scripts, but we all need to find new and creative ways of showing weak, flawed characters without having to resort to name-calling or stereotypes.

There are plenty of comedians who are defined as "offensive" these days – Jimmy Carr, Frankie Boyle, Ricky Gervais, Jim Davidson. Unlike Jerry, they have earned this label through carefully curated TV careers. Every now and then someone complains about their live shows, or about something they say on TV. Each side stands up to defend or attack said comedian, depending on how their own personal beliefs correspond with the political position of the comic. Each "controversial" debate further boosts the profile of said comedian.

In the 1990s Jim Davidson and Benny Hill were sacked by ITV, because their humour was considered out of step with what the big advertisers deemed to fit with their image. Davidson, ironically, moved to the BBC and enjoyed a long career there. Nobody called it 'woke' or 'cancel culture'. In those days, it was called 'free market economics.'

Nowadays it's defined through a prism of politics, although the economics of the issue are the same. Ricky Gervais's recent comments on the trans issue were either spot on or transphobic depending which side you support. But the people who attacked him did more to promote the TV special they came from than any other publicity.

We know who these comics are. As the saying goes, if you don't like it, you can switch off. Ricky Gervais is no more expecting trans supporters to come to his gigs than Frankie Boyle would expect the presence of Tories. Those guys don't have to worry about offending audiences, they already have their own tribes. What about you?

In recent years comedy writers and performers have negotiated issues of political correctness by many different means. There are the sexist and racist character creations of writer-performers, 21st century Alf Garnetts we are supposed to laugh *at*, not *with*. Then there are those characters that writers used to get away with calling "stupid", or "the free laugh" as a former co-writer of mine used to call them.

Nowadays the latter would be recognised instantly as people with learning difficulties such as dyslexia or high functioning autism. In recent years there have been characters who have addressed those difficulties head on. Moss in The IT Crowd and Sam in the Netflix series Atypical are two examples. Writers have worked hard to represent such characters in a funny yet sympathetic manner. Not always successfully.

Members of the neurodivergent community are beginning to protest that these characters have been written by people who have not been diagnosed with autism themselves. And in the coming years we'll see more writers from these communities, just as we've seen more members of diverse ethnic groups joking about their lived experiences.

This was a problem for many years as white male writers tried to write scripts about characters from ethnic backgrounds or with disabilities. Or even, gasp, women! The arguments continue and the statistics still show that most comedy is written by white males. But for the first time in four decades of battling on behalf of my union The Writers' Guild for more diverse voices at the writing stage, I've noticed that things are slowly changing. Too slowly for some, but change they are.

ITV continues to react to the views of its advertisers, and the diversity of their shows is beginning to reflect that. Netflix demands that any company pitching them ideas reflects as close as possible the ethnic make-up of the country they're coming from. We are no longer surprised by shows featuring disabled performers or wait nervously for pronouncements about comedies introducing ethnic minorities in lead roles.

In the last book I went in deep and personal with my views on political jokes. I looked at that chapter and decided that there was almost nothing that I said there that could move the arguments forward or help people to become better comedy writers. Whatever my opinions, someone reading will counter with the opposite and nothing will move forward. But I think the last couple of paragraphs might be useful:

I'm never going to stop you from writing what you want. And if you're challenging a consensus viewpoint you will inevitably upset people on the way. Mel Brooks talked of The Producers as the film he assumed had killed his Hollywood career for good.

35 years later it was a massive hit on Broadway. Its success has endured because behind the bad taste jokes, it's making a serious, universally accessible point about Nazism.

If you want to write edgy or dark, make sure you have a reason other than "I'm deliberately trying to annoy the politically correct brigade".

SUMMARY

You either think political correctness has gone too far. Or it hasn't gone far enough.

Political correctness goes in cycles. Most cancellations of shows or turning down of older performers are to do with market forces. Occasionally shows are cancelled because of the offence they cause to powerful pressure groups.

This makes it tricky for you, starting out on your comedy writing career, to navigate what can and can't be said.

Tricky, but not impossible.

Don't be afraid to express controversial opinions. Be prepared to back them up with your own moral viewpoint.

Part Five
An Introduction To Rewriting

All writing is rewriting.

No – scrap that...

What I mean is...

Anyway-

32

...Is Rewriting Is Writing Is Re...

There are approximately one million nine hundred and sixty three thousand books out there telling you how to write a script. As far as I can see there are only two about rewriting.

One of them is Making A Good Script Great by Linda Seger. Which is not about rewriting! It's about going back to the beginning and getting everything in place *before* you start the first draft *ahead* of rewriting it. In other words, it's yet ANOTHER book about how to write the first draft.

What is the best approach to rewriting? The first is to think of it not so much as the next phase after you've written your script, but part of a constant, ongoing process.

Let's go right back to the beginning. You suddenly have a great idea. You must write it down straight away. The jumble of words or light bulb thought that entered your head is turned into a written sentence.

It's only seconds since you had the idea and already you are reshaping it.

Rewriting begins at almost exactly the same time as writing.

Sometimes the finished product doesn't happen until seconds before it is first performed live. If rewriting up to five minutes before curtain-rising was good enough for Shakespeare, it's good enough for you.

Second, remind yourself that no first draft is ever good enough. It's called "the vomit draft" for a reason. Get everything out there, including all the stuff you know you'll never use.

Prepare and prepare and prepare. Know a lot of what you're going to write before you commit to the script – but appreciate that there is more work to be done. You won't always know what to change when you embark on a rewrite. But there will be moments when writing your first draft where you will say to yourself "here's something that I know isn't quite right – I'll try and come back and fix it later." Make a note – a written note – that you can come back to.

Third, be wary of too much advice. Over the last year there have been approximately one million nine hundred and sixty-three thousand articles in newspapers advising Keir Starmer how to beat the Tories. If he followed everyone's counsel, he'd be doing one thing today and the opposite tomorrow until 2093.

Not everyone will look at your script and agree about what needs to change. Some people, script professionals even, will directly contradict each other. Go back to all that planning and preparing you did at the start of writing, then go with your gut.

However – and this is the great get-out clause for the writing coach – rewriting doesn't always make it better. "You told me to change that, Dave! And now you say it's worse!"

I didn't *tell* you to change that. I *suggested* you might consider changing it.

It might be a tiny thread that's not working, but like a faultily knitted sweater unpicking may cause the whole thing to vanish in front of your eyes.

Enough about why you need to do it. Next question is, how do you rewrite?

Every script is different, and every script I look at will require different solutions.

Linda Seger says you should only re-write what isn't working and leave the rest alone. How can you know?

There are a million reasons why scripts go wrong. Each has its own faulty DNA. There are three crucial ways in which most scripts nearly always fail, and your first draft may have one of these, or elements of all three:

- Your stories lack high stakes.

- The characters are not driving your stories.

- Your world is not clear.

Return to your old friend of those original 25 words, that you used to describe your idea in Chapter 2. Ask yourself these questions – and these are questions you are asking yourself every day, at every stage of the process, because all writing is rewriting:

Do you have one or possibly two characters driving the story through their actions? Are they making things worse? Is this because of a fundamental flaw in their personalities? Are they making things so bad, that around about three quarters of the way through their world is about to fall apart?

If you're writing a sitcom, are they back where they were at the start?

Before you even think of rewriting, read the script to yourself in one go – or if you're really lucky get a bunch of actors to read it for you. Leave your ego at the door and imagine it's the work of someone else, someone you are not emotionally invested in.

You'll hear where it's stumbling, which jokes work and which fall into the ether. How your big idea is moving forward, or even if you have a big idea.

Accept that your second draft is as necessary as your first, there was always going to be a second draft even as you finished the first draft and thought you couldn't make it any better.

In fact once you consider the whole process, the journey from "I've had an idea" to "Coming up on BBC2, your show" – you'll see that the second draft is the next small step in making you a better writer. I'd like to become so good that I don't have to repeat myself but it's no use. For the third time I'll remind you that all writing is rewriting.

There is almost no writing about rewriting. Which is ridiculous if you think about it. Everything you've ever read, or watched at the movies or on TV, has been through several rewrites. Yet the dream you're being sold that you can become a writer, is framed only within the context of its opening stages.

Imagine being told that the key to becoming a really good plumber is to own a monkey wrench, and every single book about plumbing tells you how to use it. That's going to get you so far, but you need more. And if you think that's a crap metaphor, well I do too but at the moment I haven't got time to think of a better one and rewrite it.

Which brings me to the first point about rewriting. The most successful writing is where the writer has worked hardest to eliminate everything they believe isn't working. No one ever knows if a piece of writing is going to be successful until it encounters an audience. At which point, it can't be changed. All that we *can* know is that we worked and worked and worked on that script, or novel or screenplay, we examined every story, every character action, every sentence until there wasn't a word we wouldn't fight to keep.

If you can't know for sure what difference the rewriting will make, how then can you hope to improve your work?

The answer is to return to the effort you put in at the very early stage of developing your idea.

Let's go back to Chapter 2. Think about the answers you gave to those questions when this idea was nothing more than a jumble of thoughts in your head.

1. What's it about?

A person. The world. A goal. The obstacle.

As you go through the process of your first draft it's easy to get carried away by a new thought and forget what your original idea was about.

This is not a bad thing. It may be brilliant. It may be the breakthrough that allows you to push forward. But what you must do before you continue is revisit that initial premise and change it accordingly. Otherwise, you may find that you're writing two different manuscripts: the one that has moved on your initial idea and you're all excited about, and the one that originally inspired you.

There's nothing wrong with a show being about lots of things, but that anchor has to be one thing. The clue is often in the title: Father Ted. Miranda. Dad's Army. "In this week's episode of Miranda, the whole story is about mum's new boyfriend." Promising idea, you can see where the jokes will come, but unless it's all about Miranda it isn't an episode of that show.

2. What's it really about?

Whichever cliché you have gone with, you should have it written on a post-it note that you can see every moment you're writing.

3. Who's it about?

This is the most common problem I come across with first draft scripts. We don't know who the main character is, or characters are. And even when we do, we don't know why they are that main character. While writing your first draft, ask yourself: in this scene I'm writing, is my protagonist chasing one of their main goals? If they're not, you're writing the wrong scene.

4. Where in the world?

Your script needs to be anchored. You can go anywhere, especially on radio and in novels. You can travel to new planets or ancient historical times or 26 different flight destinations, as in the 26 separate episodes of Cabin Pressure, one of the finest radio sitcoms ever.

Unless I know where you're starting from in Act One Scene One, chances are I'll get lost in the middle of the script. And so will you.

5. Why me?

I always feel slightly awkward asking strangers to investigate the darkest recesses of their lives. I'm not a therapist. But is there something in your script, a self-awareness in your writing that shows up as lack of self-awareness in your character? Or are you still holding back?

6. Why now?

Chances are a period of several months has passed since you first asked this question of your work. What has changed in that time? When I started rewriting this chapter, Boris Johnson was still Prime Minister and Elizabeth was our Queen. That was 48 hours ago. This isn't about being topical or predicting the immediate future, but you need to have a sense that the issues you're dealing with, the new way of looking at a familiar idea, is still relevant to what you've written so far.

Learning how to rewrite is a similar process to learning how to write. The more you do it, the better you should become. That means you should try and write every day. I've swung back and forth on this hoary old piece of writing advice, advocating it in the book before last, disagreeing with that in my next book and now, I'm back to the "write daily" mantra.

That doesn't mean "write a chapter of your book every day", it's about establishing a habit. Finding 10 minutes – or 15 if you can – every day, to sit, and let your thoughts run free. What's the problem with your script? You don't know? Write that down. Is there a way I can make this script better? This character funnier? Why can't I think of answers to this? Even writing down why you can't write is writing.

Writing every day, preferably at the same time, turns an emotional desire into a professional habit. It helps to diminish the baggage of expectation we bring to the blank page, when the idea of "being a writer" can seem so overwhelming that it can make you want to give up and go back to stamp collecting or scuba diving.

Last time you looked that first draft was so perfect there wasn't a single word you needed to change. Now you're ready to work on it from a fresh perspective. Probably best not to go at it with a monkey wrench.

SUMMARY

All writing involves rewriting.

First draft? Worst draft.

The three most common mistakes I see in first drafts:

Your stories lack high stakes. The characters are not driving your stories. Your world is not clear.

Ask yourself the questions you asked at the start of the process.

What's it about? What's it really about? Who's it about? Where in the world? Why me? Why now?

33
Plotting – The Final Journey

I left you at the end of Chapter 16 in suspense. All was lost for our main character. Everything that could possibly go wrong had gone wrong. The only conceivable outcomes were humiliation, destitution, isolation, pain, death. Given that this is supposed to be a comedy, we'll stick with humiliation.

One reason many of our scripts have problems is because we don't always follow the plotting-by-numbers formula I outlined earlier. But even if you have made it to this all-is-lost moment, here are a few reasons why the way you resolve this final twist isn't quite working:

1 You used a crowbar

I see this a lot in otherwise carefully crafted scripts. Writing that first draft fuelled by inspiration and instinct, you powered your way through 20 minutes of fun and jokes.

You knew there had to be a twist near the end. At which point, a big problem suddenly occurred for the protagonist. All was lost! Ah, I'll just gently prise the script open and insert a funny solution here. Sorry, we can see the join. It's not working Scooby! Only the character can save your plot!

2 You introduced a new character late on

You might argue that this is a character who will feature more over the course of the rest of the series.

No disrespect, but if you're reading this my guess is you have not yet been commissioned to write the next five episodes. This is a one-off script whose aim is to sell you as a potential professional writer. There are thousands of you after the same limited number of slots. For your script to stand out we need to see everything you can do, and now.

THE COMPLETE COMEDY WRITER

3 You failed to escalate

Something bad happened to your character, better still they made it happen because of their character flaw. Another bad thing happened, and they dealt with that.

And another. You kept my interest, but you weren't leading that character deeper into the big black hole they're meant to be digging themselves into.

4 You left those loose ends untied

I see this a lot, even watching shows by the best TV writers.

Because our comedy characters are often loveable losers who never learn from their mistakes, it's possible to reach that point of no return, where everything has gone disastrously wrong, and for our lead character to shrug their shoulders. They stand in the midst of destruction and humiliation around them and say, "what a fool I've been."

The credits roll, it's okay, we'll be back next week and there'll be another episode where the same can happen.

True, but the audience might not join you again. If you're not interested in getting your characters out of the hole you spent 20 minutes digging for them, why should we be? If you're wondering why some TV shows last many series more than others – Only Fools and Horses, Brooklyn 99, Not Going Out, Modern Family – one of the reasons is the writers have worked that little bit harder to tie up the loose ends.

5 You ran out of steam

If a script makes the long list of a competition, it's usually because the first ten pages are great. This list is usually shortened because many of those scripts run out of energy as they continue.

There is something to be said for the Splurge School of Writing,

189

especially when you're writing something as relatively short as
a half hour sitcom, usually around 5000 words. Get it all down,
now. But at some point you're going to have to fix those holes.
Better to have considered them before you start writing.

6 You added more twists

This is a common fault in all areas of comedy writing. It's
tempting. Sometimes, in the hands of the greats, it works
beautifully. The Good Place, Michael Schur's philosophy follow
up to the wackier hits Brooklyn 99 and Parks and Rec,
occasionally made you gasp with delight. Other times the show
almost collapsed under the weight of its tangential shifts.

It's hard, really hard, to find a plausible way to navigate a path
to the end of the episode. Maybe if I add a new twist here that
will offer me a new solution. Sorry, it won't. Stick to your story.

How then, are you to make it from "all is lost or won" to "The
End"?

The specific answer is different for every piece of work. The
general answer is, always, your main character.

For this to be the case, you need to have put in those dull boring
hours of staring into space, thinking you've found a new twist
to an old type. What I described in the last chapter of
eliminating as many options as you can. You've tested the
character, found your solutions wanting, and tried again.

You might still not find the perfect solution.

How is it possible to provide a better conclusion to your story?

1 Your heroine learns the wrong thing

Sitcom characters never learn, as we never tire of saying. But
sometimes they learn the wrong thing. Next time, Basil decides,
Sybil won't find out. I will lie better.

I don't want to give away too much of the story in the follow-up to my first novel Stand Up, Barry Goldman. But him learning the wrong thing will hopefully make you want to read the final book in the trilogy. All that remains is for me to write it.

2 They learn but they forget

In every episode of Not Going Out there is a scene at the end with Lee and Lucy together on the sofa, alone. When I was writing on the show these were the hardest scenes to work on, because they were the same every week.

The point was for Lucy to say to Lee "what have you learned from your stupidity this week?" and Lee to answer: "I have learned that I behaved very stupidly. I'll try not to do it again." Seconds later something new will happen and he will act stupidly again.

Occasionally this would be as a joke to prove he had learned his lesson for now. Other times he will have forgotten from the point where he learned from his mistake to the end of the scene, barely a minute of real time.

3 They act out of character

You may get away with doing this very occasionally, once a series at the most. But if you do it too often you will lose the clarity of characterisation and confuse your audience. And, as James Cary always says, "confusion is the enemy of comedy."

4 They are saved by events

This is sometimes called deus ex machina which literally means your plot is saved by a god manipulating your story from a machine.

Or as we might also say "a cop-out".

I remember a beautifully brilliant one used by Guy Jenkin in an episode of Life On Mars. Sam Tyler is chained to a lathe and in the classic style of 60s and 70s movies a giant saw is working its way up the middle and will cut him in half. With the rotating blades millimetres away from Sam's genitalia, the machine stops, and the lights go out. A power cut.

For those of us old enough to remember the electricity strike of 1973, it was a brilliant reminder of how the regulated power cuts occasionally caught us out in mid-use of an electric device. Guy's dazzling use of real events was the exception that proves the rule.

5 The wrong thing turns out to be the right thing

Phil Dunphy's attempts to be Superdad in Modern Family always go wrong, but they send him to a dark place where for a moment, he lashes out against the people he loves. It's a jolt to them, and us watching, because the jolly mask has dropped and it's an ugly sight.

But it shows us he's human. He does bad things for good reasons, and we always forgive him for exposing that vulnerability. He's usually forgotten by the time the credits run over the final scene, ready to return next week, annoyingly cheery as ever.

6 I get knocked down, but I get up again

Every week Father Ted comes up with a scheme to escape Craggy Island. Every week he fails, due to his own character flaws. He will not be broken.

I'm sure there are more, but I've run out of time. Maybe I haven't put in enough work to come up with them. If you can think of other examples of how characters get back to where they were at the start of the episode, I'd love to hear from you.

Meantime if you want to fix that plot, you're going to have to fix your character.

SUMMARY

You can get a long way through a draft, writing by the seat of your pants. At some point you're going to have to find a plausible, creative, satisfying path to the end.

Before you get to the end of the first draft, be sure to have put in the slog on your outline. You can't make it perfect, but you can protect against having too many holes.

Look closely at the journey from "all is lost" to "the end". Have you tried to add something new? Have you let the story drift? Have you confused "all is lost" with "the end"?

Look for solutions from your characters. Look back at what you made them do earlier. See how their flaws can get them not just into scrapes, but out of them too.

Whatever the question is about fixing your script, the answer is invariably: the character.

34

Press Send- Wait for It!

There's always a good reason to not send that manuscript. To decide at the last minute that it's not good enough. Unless someone's paying you to write it. In which case, the luxury of perfection tomorrow is denied you.

If it's too late to manage that drastic rewrite you now realise is required, can you at least salvage the first ten pages? A reader blown away by your opening will give you a lot of leeway for the rest of the manuscript.

I often read the first ten pages of new scripts and attend showcase performances of the opening ten minutes of comedy shows by new authors. Nothing beats the terror and excitement of seeing your words performed in front of an audience. You can blame the actors all you want but you'll need a better excuse when you watch the audience and they're not laughing.

When I read the first ten pages, one of the most frequent issues is that the main character or characters barely feature. When I mention this to writers, they say things like "Well, that scene isn't the main setting and those aren't the main characters."

I'm sure there are plenty of movies and novels where we don't meet the main character until several pages in, but I can't think of one. Perhaps when you're an established writer you'll be granted permission to play with the form and subvert our expectations. The people that you require to read your current magnum opus will be expecting to know who and what it's about as soon as possible. They'll have decided after ten pages whether they want to continue.

As binge-watching becomes the norm it's more important than ever to ensure that your audience know what they're dealing with as soon as possible. Even if it's "this show makes no sense at all... yet-" that at least kept me watching Russian Doll.

Whatever you're writing, you need to make a strong impression in your opening. Given that a car chase or exploding building will only tell your reader that you've used the entire budget for the movie in your first minute, what else can you do to hold their attention?

Every script or story you write must have as much of the following as possible in the first ten pages. I'd go further and say that when you're creating a show or novel series with new and hopefully returning characters, and fresh stories, you should have these somewhere in every chapter or scene.

The main character should be one of the most compelling reasons for you wanting to write. You've come up with a creature so original, and so funny, you want them to be around as much as possible. Everything that happens will revolve around them.

The main premise is the underlying theme. Thought I should mention that it's not this week's episode. It's usually defined by the flaws in the main character, or them trying to be something they're not. It's not enough to say "I want to write a sitcom about a bloke who runs a hotel": you want to show a bloke doing a job whose character makes him thoroughly and perfectly unsuited to it. In case you've forgotten, the premise is different from the opening chapter or start of the episode.

The opening chapter or start of the episode is the big moment that kickstarts the action. It needs to begin as soon as possible. Syd Field told you that. Something has to happen to your main character. A crisis, or an opportunity. Whatever genre you're writing in, there should be someone, or a couple of people, in pursuit of something they don't have, or may not even know they want, yet. In the opening ten pages, and throughout, we want to see them plotting to get it. In sitcom we already know they will fail at the end, but we return each week because we want to know how they're going to fail next time around.

And it should be a **life-changing moment**. If you're lucky enough to have actors trying out your script, think of how much you can stretch them to give their best performance. How big is that "something happens" moment? Your actor would love it to be potentially life changing.

The "world" can be any combination of factors like the location, the "rules of engagement" between characters - for instance we can tell during any scene between Miranda and her mum what their relationship is like. Familiar landmarks will help add layers of meaning to the show.

If you're writing a comedy set in a warzone, such as M*A*S*H (which began as a novel, then became a movie, then a sitcom) or Bluestone 42; whatever else is going on, you know that everyone is aware they could be killed at any time. This is a great setting for gallows humour, people can be as rude as they like to everyone else. Fear of the common enemy is bigger than any arguments they may have with each other.

Watch out for **people talking**. At the last showcase I attended I saw lots of good performing of funny jokes. We all like jokes, I can't repeat enough how often we forget to put jokes in our scripts. If your work consists of people talking in jokey conversations and little else, you might as well be writing for a panel show.

I make no apologies for repeating here what's been said elsewhere. However much you're told the same piece of information, there's always a struggle to make it stick.

Finally, here are a few thoughts that seem to contradict each other. Yet all can be contained in one great script.

First, think big. One of the live episodes I watched was a sitcom about a hostage situation. The premise was clever and there were funny twists along the way.

Remember, though, that characters drive stories. Even the most gripping hostage movie can be enhanced when we take a moment out of the breath-taking action to examine the minutiae of the lives of those involved.

Don't let big distract you too much. One of my favourite sitcoms in recent years was Dead Boss, in which Sharon Horgan's character had been wrongfully arrested. The main story was about trying to get her out of prison. The characters were all great and the prison sections worked well. However the story outside was so different – it lacked the conflict and confinement of prison and crucially, it lacked the show's star Sharon Horgan – that it ended up being two different spectacles.

Second, big doesn't always mean size. The best showcase opening I saw was a small gentle one, involving a young woman whose partner had died. It had emotional depth, humour and pathos.

Big or small, there must always be at least one new thing. There's a lot of contradiction going on in this chapter (or is there?) which is exactly how it should be.

If everything I said was right, then I'd be far too busy writing episode 250 of my international sitcom hit to be doing this now. There's nothing wrong with pitching another sitcom set in a police station if you can make it as dazzling and yet different in one way to Brooklyn 99.

I read a lot of scripts by twentysomething male writers about a bunch of twentysomething blokes whose lives are going nowhere. I accept that I am having a go at you for trying to come up with the next Friends or Slackers. Those worked because they brought something new to a familiar setting. Another favourite sitcom of mine of recent times was Lovesick, about a twentysomething bloke whose life was going nowhere.

I'm hoping you'll be so busy trying to get all the above into your opening ten pages that you won't have space for that other staple of every doomed script I've ever read: backstory.

Backstory is the enemy of comedy. What was David Brent doing before he became the boss at Wernham Hogg? How did he get that job? I don't know. How did Jez and Mark in Peep Show first meet? I don't care.

There is a reason writers put backstory into their scripts, and it's because they believe, mistakenly, that we need to set up the story to understand who the characters are. But we don't. There are three Catholic priests and a housemaid trapped on a remote island as far away from humanity as it's possible to be.

We don't need to know how they got there, it's the Catholic church and we can all hazard a few guesses. Our enjoyment of Father Ted is not harmed by our lack of this knowledge.

The other reason people add backstory is because it's part of the groundwork you put in before you wrote a single word of your story. You don't want to waste it.

In movies and novels, backstory has a place, but not in the first ten pages. It works best when it teases out the reasons your character failed to resolve whatever problem you threw at them at the end of Act One. The best use of backstory comes when it's a surprise, even when it was there all the time. Brooklyn by Colm Tóibín is not a comedy, and not the liveliest read or movie, but there is one moment in the story you so don't see coming that is both profoundly shocking and totally believable.

Too often it is the convenient fallback to pull the writer out of a tricky plot situation they have created for themselves. This is always unsatisfying, and invariably the fault of a writer who has not worked hard enough to create a believable, compelling character.

I'm going to tell you how I came to write this book.

In 2008, the stand-up comedy website Chortle began running a page called Correspondents, where people were invited to write anything they wanted about comedy. I read a few articles and thought this was something I could probably do quite well.

I wrote more articles until in 2013 I decided to adapt what I'd already written and turn it into a book. I still love writing about comedy, and over the course of the next few years I developed ideas that have finally turned into this book. There have been so many changes to the world of comedy since it came out that I decided to update it.

See how boring those last two paragraphs were? Backstory? Bin it.

****

Now it's time to wave goodbye to your darling, the most recent love of your life, press that button and send your beautiful, perfect-as-it'll-ever-be collection of carefully crafted words fluttering out onto the superhighway. They say that loving your babies is knowing when to let go.

Time to begin work on your next idea.

SUMMARY

Ready to send off your work? Look again at the opening. Can you make it brilliant?

Make sure everything that matters to the rest of story is embedded in those opening pages: character, premise, plot, world.

And something big needs to happen. We need to see that, and the start of the consequences, in the opening couple of chapters or first ten pages.

No backstory here please. Save it for later – or bin it.

Press send.

Start a new project.

Good luck!

Part Six
Beyond Writing

Five years ago I decided I wanted to be a novelist. I went further, decided I wanted to be A Novelist.

What's the difference? In my complete ignorance I imagined this world where I'd be invited to Edinburgh to talk to hundreds of adoring fans about how I had singlehandedly revived the Great British Comic Novel. Wodehouse, Sharp, Townsend, Cohen. I dared to dream. Luckily, I never said any of this out loud.

Five years later, I can say "I am a novelist." I have a novel out, two more on the way. Am I a making a living at it? Course not! Those dreams of five years ago were the dreams of an ignorant man. I knew so little I didn't even know what I didn't know.

I've learned through a process of trial and error, mostly error, that I probably never will make a living at it. But as long as I continue to derive such pleasure from writing novels, I'll carry on.

What I wish I'd had five years ago was something that might have helped me avoid some of the biggest pitfalls, that might have given a shape and order to the process, may have got me further down the line, quicker. A version of this book, I guess.

If you've decided you want to be a comedy writer, congratulations! You're where I was five years ago.

You probably think five years is a fair amount of time to give yourself to see if you can make a living at it. You may be right.

At some point, a map will be useful. However, several walking holidays in the Lake District have taught me that even with a detailed Ordnance Survey guide, you can still spend hours getting lost in the woods.

This book isn't a map, more a collection of signposts. I can't promise it's going to get you to where you want to be, but I can point you in the right direction.

You've written your work. Maybe have a portfolio. Sitcoms, novels, kids shows, TV pilots, screenplays.

Now what?

35
Would Like to Meet

Frank Muir and Denis Norden. Ray Galton and Alan Simpson. Clement and La Frenais, French and Saunders, Armstrong and Bain. It's no coincidence that since the start of radio and TV comedy, there have always been hugely successful writing partnerships.

Norden said you need two people when you're writing comedy, one to type and one to stare out the window.

I've written alone and in partnerships, been typer and starer. I enjoy writing alone but writing with a partner is way more fun.

I've been giggling to myself for weeks about a joke I wrote for something that's a year from happening. I'm desperate to share but it's not funny out of context. I needed to have someone in the room when I thought of it. Not least because if they hadn't found it funny, I'd have had to consider binning it.

You don't get the same in drama. When Jed Mercurio builds to an exciting climax in episode 83 of Line of Duty, he doesn't have someone else in the room cowering in the corner to validate that the thing he just thought of is scary enough.

When it comes to topical programmes, having a writing partner is especially helpful. Many of the producers I've worked with over the years met me for the first time in the corridors of BBC Radio Comedy where Week Ending was made.

Ian Brown and James Hendrie, who have together written hundreds of sitcom episodes for radio and TV, met there. Baddiel and Newman began their partnership writing for that show. I met Pete Sinclair there in 1983. 39 years later we're still good friends and occasionally write together.

With the BBC having to cut back on training new writers, where else can you go to meet the co-writer of your dreams?

If you're in London there's London Comedy Writers (londoncomedywriters.com). Do you need to be in London? The BBC have long pioneered attempts to move the centre of comedy gravity from London to the regions. Scotland, Wales, Northern Ireland and Manchester all now have growing comedy departments. Channel 4 is planning to move more programme making to Leeds.

Any reticence to creating our working relationships online has been swept away by the pandemic.

Nowadays the most obvious places to meet a partner are the British Comedy Guide (comedy.co.uk) and The Comedy Crowd (thecomedycrowd.com). For a small annual fee you can join BCG Pro and find a ton of resources, while Comedy Crowd hold frequent meetings (still currently online) for new writers.

In both cases you're going to have to do some detective work to find like-minded people. Even when you meet someone, you might struggle to hit it off initially. I suggest you come together to work on a single project. It could be writing jokes for a series of Breaking the News, or coming up with ideas for The Skewer. Or entering a sitcom/sketch writing competition with a closing date that's a few months away.

A lot of people talk about writing partnerships like they're marriages, or dating. And there are similarities. Working with one partner I sometimes spent more time with him than my wife. And many of your conversations can be quite revealing and intimate.

In the early stages of the partnership, it's more businesslike. Which is good. Imagine you're looking for a shop to buy a loaf of bread. You might not like the first place you go, but you're not then going to say "That's it! I'm through with yeast products. From now on I'm sticking to Ryvita."

If it doesn't work out, it's okay to move on. There's plenty more fish in the surrealist joke book.

Let's say you agree, after your initial chat, to give it a go. What should you do?

Sign a contract It's not a formal contract. Initially it's for a single project. It can be an email. As long as you've written something down that both have agreed on. Beyond agreeing to split your earnings and costs 50-50, there's not a lot else at this stage. And then it does become like dating.

If after that one project you enjoyed the process then by all means have another meeting and discuss if you want to work more.

Be realistic I remember the first time Lee Evans met Stuart Silver, who went on to become his co-writer for many decades. I remember because I was there. A few of us were, writing for a TV show for Lee. It was love at first sight. Lee was a generous person in the room, but it soon became obvious that this was different. This was the start of something big, and the rest of us were mere spectators in this comedy writers rom com.

The reason I remember it so vividly is because it's the only time I've ever seen that happen. It was the summer of 1990 and here were two people approaching the peak of their successful careers. Be realistic about where your partnership may be going...

...But dare to dream I have seen how in topical writing that two heads are often twice as good as one. In the Week Ending days if a writer was struggling with a sketch as the deadline approached he'd often ask someone in the room to come and sit with him. Yes it was always a he back then.

Often the problem was simple enough, it just needed another comedy brain to fix. If you can find ways to complement each other's writing you can move ahead in this business pretty quickly.

Talk about your strengths and weaknesses Ahead of working together it's worth discussing openly what you believe these to be. Sometimes you don't know until you start writing with a partner. You may think you're good at something, but the partner might be better. Or the opposite. Either way it's good to have a little vulnerability out in the open. You need to be able to say "sorry I didn't find that line funny" without the other person thinking "you know nothing!" and "I hate you!"

Work with your differences and similarities Often the similarities can be what brings you together. Pete and I shared interests, a similar sense of humour and similar attitudes to rewriting. I thought I was quite thorough at rewriting, but Pete was way ahead of me in that field. I think I may have tried to compete with him in the early days but soon let him loose, leaving other areas for me to concentrate on.

Enjoy other people's contributions to your ideas One of the big problems I used to have in writing rooms was lack of confidence. I didn't always like to shout out. Sometimes I thought of a line but judged myself and held it in. Seconds later someone else would say it and get the credit. Other times I would say it, and the man with the louder voice would run with it and claim it as his own.

This is something I know a lot of women struggle with, one of the reasons why it has taken so long for comedy writers' rooms in the UK to move into the 21st century, out of the 19th.

When you're writing with a partner you can enjoy coming up with an idea and watching them run with it. And vice versa. You are a single unit, no one is proprietorial.

Enjoy working with others towards a common goal It's good to accept we can't do everything ourselves. We need to recognise our limitations. And it's always a good feeling to be with someone who's got your back.

Have fun

Bear in mind that when you're writing with a partner you're earning half as much as when you're on your own. Of course it's hard work as well, but be sure to enjoy the experience.

SUMMARY

If you're writing for radio or the screen, you might want to consider working with a comedy partner.

The money's not so good, but it's way more fun.

It's a bit like dating. Don't expect to find your dream partner on day one. You'll find out quicker if your jokes work.

Usually if you can make the other person laugh, it goes in the script.

36

Network to Get Work

Earlier I dealt with one of the three questions I'm asked most frequently by new writers. "Where do you get your ideas from?"

I don't plan to handle question two at this point - "which typeface font should I write my scripts in?" - but number three merits a response.

"How do I get an agent?"

The simple answer I gave for many years was "Write a brilliant script". Left it there. It's in the first edition.

There are two problems with this. First, most of what we write is not brilliant. Some of it is good, some mediocre, and some awful. When you're starting out, it's reasonable to say that while you may be showing promise, it's unlikely that your script will be brilliant.

Second, and this is a more recent development, it has become almost impossible for unrepresented writers to get their scripts into the hands of people they want to represent them.

How do we resolve this Catch 22, which applies across the industry regardless of your creative endeavour?

Let's start by playing a pointless Twitter game called "take a question and remove one word from it," and ask instead:

"Do I get an agent?"

The answer is, not necessarily. Agents perform several great tasks for writers. They dig through the deep weeds of your contract. Make sure you're getting the best deal. They know when producers are looking for writers on new shows and will ensure your name is added to their list. They help set up meetings. Give you credibility. "Call my agent" isn't only a fab French TV show, it's a phrase you can utter that tells the listener that you should be taken seriously.

The one thing agents rarely do is get you work. If a producer wants you for a job they'll find you somehow, but they'll probably contact your agent first. If they want someone like you, they'll let you know via your agent. There's no guarantee that the job is yours.

Instead of expending too much energy in this direction, you can choose not to worry about getting an agent and crack on with writing your not-quite-brilliant-yet script.

If you want a specific agent, the chances are that they won't want you. You want them because they look after great people you love, which means they're probably too busy to take on new clients. That said, my own agent represents some of the busiest and most successful writers I know, but also follows the competitions entered by new writers and takes on the best of them.

If you decide to hold off at this point from getting an agent, what else can you do?

For this next section I am greatly indebted to Danny Stack, one half of UK Scriptwriters and one of the most inspiring influences on my career since I started teaching around 15 years ago.

Danny appears more prominently in the next chapter but recently he ran a great thread on Twitter explaining what you need to do to become a professional writer.

Write the brilliant script, of course. That's the given. Your next step is to look at where most of the paid writing work is for new writers.

That's the place where you need to be networking.

Get meetings. You can do it. Put your scripts out there. It can be done. Pick up knowledge of your industry. It's not difficult.

Who do you know? Write out a list. You'll be surprised. There are people you don't know whose presence online makes them an email away. British Comedy Guide, The Comedy Crowd, Chortle. Websites devoted exclusively to comedy. Don't bombard them but if you want to find out some useful information don't be afraid to establish polite contact.

Others you don't know have a presence on social media. Don't barge in, but again, don't be afraid to ask intelligent questions. And if you're going to be on social media, think about how you can be present. Write topical jokes if you can. Be a funny interesting person. See what observations people are making and search for a different angle.

Watch and listen. Take a note of every show you have seen or listened to that you like. Find out the names of everyone who worked on those shows – writers, producers, executive producers, script editors.

What's the best way to approach producers? Start with the small BBC departments that are known to encourage new writers – radio and kids' TV. It's a small industry, and while it's incredibly hard to get anything made, there are a few useful gatekeepers left at the BBC.

Again, these producers are only an email away. It's not difficult to find out how to contact them. If you enjoyed a show they made, tell them what you liked about it. Mention you have some scripts already written and you'd like to meet for an informal chat.

You're not asking them if they'll make your script at this stage. Not least because the answer's no. You're making a connection. You're meeting someone who can give you inside information, and who many years down the line may be able to give you work.

"Ask them questions," Danny says. "Be nice, be normal, don't be pushy or ingratiating or annoying. Above all be patient. All of this takes time."

A lot of it involves two difficult actions for the typical writer. First, it asks you to step out of your introvert shell – the thing, as we all know, that made you want to be a writer in the first place.

The second is less commented on but equally important: to think about your career as a professional. So much of what we do involves revealing our vulnerability. Even if that's not in the script, we're putting work out there knowing that we might be vilified and humiliated. No successful writer has ever gone through life without experiencing that at least once in their careers.

You must stop doing all those things we waste time on. Comparing ourselves unfavourably to successful writers we think – know – we're better than. Getting annoyed at others' success. Moaning at how bad someone else's show is.

It's time to let go of things over which you have no control. Acknowledge your negative emotions as they happen and move on in search of a more positive perspective about your career. Your job is still to write jokes, which as Denis Norden said involves making fun of others' misfortunes. But it's still a job and it requires a professional approach.

If you want to be a writer, you must participate in an industry. You may achieve your dream of quitting the day job and spending the day doing what you love. You still need to turn up at the office occasionally. Be nice to strangers. Make deals and sign contracts.

At this point, you may be ready to look for an agent.

Being a great writer is not enough. Can you work with others? Can you accept notes? Can you change and develop as others bring ideas to your work? How does an agent judge this? If they see you can work professionally with others, it's important to be able to prove that.

Most agents are looking for a mix of clients. They would love all of us to be earning six-figure book advances and so would we. Most writers, most of the time are not in that league. It could be you next year though, and if an agent sees something they really like in your writing, they'll take you on.

An agent works for you. They only make money when you make money. They aren't trying to sell your project; they're selling you as a writer.

Be aware that it's not all about you. They've got another 20 or so clients. They're under pressure to bring in big chunks of money. Offices need to be kept open. You're not going to be top priority, are you? Do you even feature in their daily thoughts? It feels personal but it isn't.

Can you quickly be stuck into a day writing on a Paddington movie? Agents need to believe in your writing, they're not just about the money.

Be honest with yourself if you're ready. Come with experience. Shows in Edinburgh, jokes regularly on topical shows, recommendations. Know what you really want to write. Look at the agents, see who specialises in what. What can you bring to the table above and beyond your promising script? Trust me, it isn't brilliant, yet. Have you got anywhere in performing or working with performers?

If there's one skill we're supposed to have as writers, it's the ability to put ourselves in someone else's shoes. Put yourself in their shoes. Agents understand how writers work but they're also businesspeople. Get your script out there and get a cut from a successful commission. How much time do they have to put in for you? Sell yourself as a business proposition.

Think of the relationship this way: How can I the writer help you? There's more to life than your agenda. Be specific about why you have chosen this agent. What can the two of you do together in the future? Maybe you don't even know. Be honest about it. Think about it. Don't be afraid to speak to more than one.

One of the best ways that you can come to the attention of an agent is to show that you are already, like your sitcom characters in Chapter 12, proactive.

If you want to become a professional writer, you need to be more than that.

You need to become a writer-hyphen.

A what? Read on...

SUMMARY

If you want to get an agent, you need to write a brilliant script.

What if your script isn't brilliant yet though? Spoiler alert: it isn't.

You don't need an agent at this point. But there are ways of meeting people in your industry.

Be patient. This takes time.

Learn more about your industry. Develop skills beyond your writing. Become a writer-hyphen.

A what? I just asked that...

37
I'll Make It Anywhere...

What's been the biggest change since I wrote the first edition of this book? Without doubt, it is the technological development that has allowed millions of people to take control over their destinies by selling their creative skills on the internet.

Whether it's making jewelry or developing online comedy sketches, content creators have found a way to market direct to the world. No expensive shop space or factory floors required, no offices or clerical staff. Just you and whatever you have in abundance that you can share with others.

I was excited by the early days of the internet. It reminded me of the start of punk rock, when a mini industry sprang up of bands recording their own songs. We made our own records, designed home-made sleeves and hawked them to the hundreds of independent record stores across the country.

Danny Stack, who I mentioned in the last chapter, was an early online pioneer. He was a beneficiary of a BBC Writersroom bursary for Irish writers in 2004. Danny began blogging soon after, when people were saying "what's blogging?" and broadband was something you used to keep your stomach in place. His tales of starting from scratch as an unknown writer in the London film world were informative and entertaining.

When I began teaching in 2006 I asked him to write a blog for me about comedy screenplays. In 2011 we ran a brief course together for scriptwriters wanting to create their own web series. It was years too early to catch on and we didn't get many takers.

But we both learned a lot about how important it is for new writers to develop additional skills for the internet age.

The writer-performer continues to dominate our comedy schedules. It started with panel shows but now the vast majority of narrative sitcom begins with the vision of an entertainer.

What does this mean if you're starting out? It's true that you are at more of a disadvantage than would have been the case 30 or 40 years ago. Comedy producers commencing their careers now like you, are spending far more time watching live comedy than reading scripts.

Many of you have no intention of appearing on stage, and why would you? For you the act of creation involves sitting alone. David Sedaris, admittedly no slouch in front of an audience, still says that for him all the action and excitement happens when he goes to sit at his desk.

Yet it's worth spending time getting to know the younger rising stars of live comedy. They may think they don't need you but they're wrong. If you like a comic or a sketch performer and feel you could write for them, it's your job to persuade them.

What I'm asking you to do is become like one of your leading characters – be proactive.

It's no longer enough to be a writer, or even a writer-performer. The problem isn't only that many performers write their own material. The very word 'writer' is being steadily diminished. Comedians know that huge numbers of their audience are unaware that material is 'written'. Punters really believe comedians walked in off the street and are saying the first thing that pops into their heads.

It's easy to see why. The compere has spent the first ten minutes asking the front row what their names are, what jobs they do, whether they are in relationships. The audience aren't going to know the compere has spreadsheets committed to memory of every joke matched to every name, occupation and relationship status of humanity.

Improvisation has helped perpetuate the myth that by shouting "Alien traffic wardens at the John Lewis make-up counter!", the audience have somehow contributed to the comedy gold that emerges occasionally from the mouths of making-it-up-as-they-go-along comic actors. We've given producers excuses to pay writers less. My least favourite producer statement is "Surely the actors will be able to come up with something on the day?"

Writers are no longer considered as vital to the process of making comedy as they were in the prime of Galton and Simpson, and Clement and La Frenais. That's wrong.

Instead of complaining we must do something about it. You're going to have to become familiar with, and participate in, the entire process of comedy creation. It's called show business for a reason, it's the business of show.

You're no longer a writer, you are a writer-performer-producer-accountant-publisher- marketing-PR.

You're going to have to become, and I can barely drag my fingers over the keys to write this hideous word, a *writerpreneur*.

I'm spending a lot of time in the world of independent publishing. Finished my first novel in March 2020 and was considering asking my agent to approach a few publishers.

I'd already assumed and happily accepted there'd be little buzz around the debut novel of another white middle-class 60something male. Then the first covid lockdown began. Every comedian I'd ever known, deprived of the oxygen of going on stage, started writing their book. I quickly waved farewell to those publisher meeting dreams.

I've nothing against rejection. We comedy writers love it, it's how we bond. Rejection is fine, it happens to our sitcom scripts all the time. But to get a book idea rejected? That's a whole new world of rebuff. There are ways out there of denting my already fragile self-esteem of which I know nothing. Was it turned down because they've got something like it in production or because it's a pile of excrement? I'm far too old to start learning now.

I have, however, late in life, discovered my inner capitalist. In the world of self-publishing, writing a book is a small part of the process. Making it yourself, designing it, proofreading, building an audience ahead of publication. Marketing, publicity, building whatever other skills you bring into the creation, all this matters.

If anything, this new model is closer to socialism. Visionary journalist Kevin Kelly predicted back in Ye Ancient Internette Era of 2006 that a thousand true fans prepared to pay us $100 a year would liberate creators from the need to go down traditional routes for exposure.

He subsequently described our urge to share content as digital socialism. Almost everything I know about independent publishing I've learned for free from podcasts, webinars, YouTube and TikTok videos. These works were all created by people who have had the experience and are sharing it to help people like me.

You coughed up a few quid for this book, but may well have arrived at that decision to purchase it having consumed hundreds of blogs, webinars and episodes of Sitcom Geeks. All available for free.

Every time I start to feel the hostility of the voice at the back of my head yelling "sell-out" and "biblio-fascist", I remind myself of the hours and weeks put into my first book, published in 2013. I stopped mentioning it a few months after it came out, because that's what I thought you did when you wrote books. I've learned that marketing, to quote Alliance of Independent Authors funder Orna Ross, is like Bob Dylan's Never Ending Tour.

You have to stop thinking of yourself as a writer. You're now a writer-producer. A writer-publisher. Work with other writer-producers as well, find people with complementary skills. Don't be afraid to keep creative control of this thing you have nurtured from nothing. Make your own stuff. You'll find out a lot quicker what works and what doesn't.

It's time to step outside of your comfort zone, stop using clichés like comfort zone, and keep writing. And producing. Editing. Formatting. Budgeting, marketing and selling.

No more carping from the sidelines. As the great writer Swift once said "haterz gonna hate hate hate hate hate but the players gonna play play play play play."

SUMMARY

Never mind the old gatekeepers. The internet has completely changed the landscape for creative people.

It's no longer enough to be a writer. You have to develop new skills.

Be proactive. Make your own stuff.

You get to retain complete control over your own projects.

Work with other writers. Find people with different skills to you.

38
...If I Can Make It There

Every September, a drained and disheveled battalion of stand-up comedians and comic actors retreat from Edinburgh back to their homes in England, broke and broken by the rigorous treadmill of performing at the Fringe.

One or two may have cracked the code and returned home in triumph, careers set for lift-off. For the rest, confronting their imagined demons and very real bank managers, they look back at four weeks of emotional devastation and decide, once and for all, that never again will they sacrifice so much demonstrative commitment in return for so little financial gain. 24 hours later, they begin working out what next year's show will be.

I've turned the epic banality of my Edinburgh experiences into a trilogy of novels that begins with Stand Up, Barry Goldman. The second and third will be published over the next year or so. I spent 11 Augusts in a row there in the 1980s and 90s, and still can't decide whether that was the most significant part of my career, or the biggest waste of time and money of my life.

The festival altered very little between then and 2019. A combination of covid, landlord greed and a growing weariness towards the polemical content of stand-up has permanently changed the landscape of the world's biggest comedy celebration.

These days there are only four options if you want to perform during the Fringe.

You can have an agent who will pay for you to go, and accept you'll be paying them back one way or another over the next 12 months; have a guaranteed well-paid job to return to in September; know someone who will put you up and put up with you for four weeks; or come from a wealthy family.

There's a fifth possibility. You can choose, as many still do, to go for broke.

I was lucky, I always had option three, and couldn't have managed without that free accommodation. Now, if I was thinking of going to Edinburgh, I'd skip a year and spend 24 months working out a brilliant show, have it ready and working within 18 months, and spend the last six months ensuring advance ticket sales would be enough to provide a cushion if it ended up sinking without trace. As many perfectly good ones often do.

Whether you're a writer, performer or combination of the two, I still think it's worth going. Doing a show every day, turning up at the same time, instils a sense of professionalism.

Being able to step back from each performance, working out what worked and what didn't, trying a new approach the next day, having a stinker but having to go back. These lessons stick with you for the rest of your life.

If it's going well, it's the best feeling in the world.

Being surrounded by thousands of people who, like you, have come here to create – yes, hopefully to get noticed too, but to be motivated to do your best. And the millions who come and watch. Not because they've been told but because they're prepared to take a chance on an unknown. It's a humbling experience.

You learn so much from being round your peers.

It forces you to think beyond your shows and develop a strategy for how to survive in comedy.

You get to meet people whose job it is to make programmes featuring people like you.

There are downsides. And these are many, beyond those mentioned at the start.

You'll be surrounded by people doing better than you. It's exhausting. There's nothing more demoralising than playing to a room where most of what you can see is empty chairs.

Bad reviews will make you feel like shit. Nobody will come up to you and talk about your good reviews, but everyone you know will have found the bad ones. Comics have developed a homing skill.

Even the good reviews will contain a word or a sentence that will irritate you. You will suffer from violent mood swings. Fall out with friends. Lose sight of why you're there, which is to get better at what you do.

What if you're a writer? What if the idea of performing fills you with absolute dread? The same rules apply, although you don't need to spend the whole four weeks there. It will still break the bank, but the potential rewards are many.

Edinburgh Fringe is an education in comedy. You'll learn more in two weeks there than a year in London. Although if you want a career in comedy, you could do a lot worse than get a place to study at Oxford or Cambridge. With the BBC no longer available as an option, the comedy halls of our high-status universities are a great training ground for the profession.

You will lose a ton of money. See a lot of crap. Feel like a gooseberry around everyone performing. You'll be intimidated by the idea that you can do this yourself. You'll be annoyed watching audiences laughing at a show that you don't find funny.

But Edinburgh Fringe is incredibly inspiring. Plan well and it won't cost you so much. You'll meet new creative partners. Learn from the best – and the worst. You'll see many examples of how to do it and how not to.

One other career option I didn't mention in the first edition of this book was the possibility of developing your craft in the United States.

For years this was considered the holy grail for top British performers – a stateside career.

Americans have always loved British humour - "Monn E Pie Thon" as they call it, and its mix of class politics and wacky surrealism. They adored the crazy sci-fi of Douglas Adams. That brainy Oxbridge crowd inspired a generation of geeky American students to develop the internet, but there was very little comedy crossover.

Three people changed the relationship between Britain and America and brought the two cultures closer. Mike Myers was born in Canada but developed his comedy in England, where his parents were born. There's a very English strand running through his most successful movie creations Wayne's World and Austin Powers, and you can see the influence take effect through the 80s and 90s editions of Saturday Night Live, America's seminal topical show.

Alternative comedy's roots were in the US. Lenny Bruce was the Godfather of stand-up who inspired generations linked not by nationality but point of view. Many Americans including Denis Leary and Steven Wright built their live careers in the UK. Eddie Izzard became the first British stand-up to cross the international divide and achieve success in the States.

It was Ricky Gervais who had the biggest impact. There had been successful non-audience sitcoms before in the UK - Spaced, The Royle Family, People Like Us and more – but nothing had such an affect across the Atlantic than the Merchant-Gervais mockumentary.

Michael Schur, who helped develop the US version of the Office and went on to co-create some of the greatest American comedy of the last two decades – Parks and Rec, Brooklyn 99, The Good Place – called the UK Office "the greatest sitcom ever."

Before The Office, most American narrative comedy was delivered in industrial quantities. Series were put together by teams of writers and sold in batches of 20 or more, which still happens. But the idea of an authored show of the kind we were used to over here, sold in six half-hour episodes, took off as a serious prospect.

All of which by way of rambling introduction suggests that there might, just might be the possibility if you're British of making a career as a comedy writer in the US.

There's more of everything in the US – more opportunities, more TV, more live shows. More people competing though. There are two possible locations, New York and LA. Although many big towns have their own comedy pedigree, including San Francisco, Chicago and Austin.

To put it simplistically, New York is the home of gag-writing, Los Angeles where the narrative happens. If you think you have the one-liner gene then the east coast is for you, otherwise head west for the Hollywood gold rush.

The same rules apply as they do to Edinburgh, multiplied several times over. Don't even think of spending time in the US unless you have big funds, a place to stay, and people you know in the business. And don't expect to pick up any work for a year. Being a performer may give you a head start but the time you take to arrange and pick up gigs won't leave you much space or energy for much else.

In other ways things are remarkably similar. Like the UK, narrative comedy has been in gradual decline, audience sitcom has all but died out and comedy drama has taken precedence. It's as hard to make it as a comedy writer as it's ever been.

But a number of British writes have achieved considerable success in the US, and our point of view is considered to have merit. Scott Dikkers founded The Onion and knows a thing or two about coming from relative obscurity to achieve great writing success in the States. He doesn't exactly recommend a move, but he does think the British are better placed than most to find their way in the American market.

"Right now," he says, "the path is very consistent, wherever you live. Put yourself out there. Get seen. Be relentless in creating stuff. Write articles. Typically the people who succeed now were seen in clubs, or as writers maybe created a funny Twitter account."

You don't have to be in New York or LA to do any of that, but if the romance appeals and bank balance allows then au revoir, and good luck!

SUMMARY

Go to the Edinburgh Festival. Plan well, and in advance.

Edinburgh is the equivalent of taking a three-year degree in How to Become a Comedy Writer.

You're going for one reason alone – to make yourself better at what you do.

There is less difference nowadays between comedy in the UK and the USA. You might consider spending time in the States.

Again, consider this part of your comedy education. Expect nothing else beyond that.

39

Know More

I sometimes spend a day in an airless room teaching people how to write comedy and am always surprised to hear myself saying things that I'd completely forgotten. The basics are simple, but it takes a lot of repeating to embed them into my stubborn mind.

Teaching, for me, is learning. I'm lucky to be podcasting about comedy writing with James Cary, the best writing teacher I know.

At various times over the years, I have attempted to make sense of that often-repeated phrase "write what you know." I've gone from saying it's meaningless to "write what you don't know" to "write what interests you".

I shan't offer yet another opinion on this topic. When it comes to the suggestion "write what you know", clearly I don't know.

All I'll say is that if you're going to take that advice, then it stands to reason that the more you know, the more you can write what you know.

James and I both create a lot of free content. You can find tons of advice from us dotted around the internet. It's not difficult. But while reading a blog or listening to a podcast, your attention might be diverted by the sound of another email pinging from your laptop, the world's second most efficient Distraction Machine after the mobile phone.

At some point, you may decide that to become a better writer you need to make a greater commitment. In recent years two practical degree courses have emerged aimed specifically at comedy writers. Both expect a level of dedication and spending of money way beyond what we've been used to.

The National Film and Television School course in Comedy Writing and Production is approaching its tenth anniversary.

The NFTS has a glamorous history of association with the British film and TV industries, and has long been shorthand to employers for "this person knows what they're doing."

If you can afford the fees, or can be helped by a bursary, it's probably worth doing. I was closely involved with the course at the start, helping senior tutor (and top radio producer) Bill Dare, interviewing candidates and tweaking the content in its early days. I see and hear of many of those interviewees succeeding in the comedy world – Charlie Dinkin, Laura Major, Daniel Audritt, Kat Butterfield, Sara Gibbs, Ed Amsden and Tom Coles, Kat Sadler. I'm sure there are more.

Would they have gone as far as they have without having taken that course? Possibly. Did their association with it help? Certainly.

Recently another radio producer Simon Nicholls created an MA in Comedy at Falmouth University. It's only been going for a couple of years so it's too early to measure its success. As far as I'm aware it's the only other course devoted specifically to comedy writing. If you can afford the time and the payments you might want to investigate.

What about a more general Creative Writing degree? There are hundreds of these, and I can't begin to offer specific advice. I taught on one a couple of years ago at Winchester University and may be doing so again. I was seriously impressed with the level of commitment and advice already offered for people wishing to work in radio and TV as writers, or as novelists.

Every student has to take a number of 12-week modules each term. I taught TV writing and the process of developing your script – and discovered a great deal myself. There are modules in movie screenplays, YA novels, crime fiction, sci-fi, self-publishing, poetry and more. It offers both a solid general education and a chance to specialize in your favourite genres.

One of the most important lessons I learned was that there are way more similarities between comedy and drama writing for

TV than there are differences. But that's a whole new book.

What if none of these useful but expensive options are open to you?

How do you teach yourself most efficiently to become a better writer?

You can start by reading more books. There are tons now, way more than any sane human can hope to read. I've read enough, I think, to at least point you towards the ones that can help you most.

Let's start specifically with comedy. Writing That Sitcom by James Cary remains the clearest book for British comedy writers. Sally Holloway's Serious Guide to Joke Writing the best practical guide. Onion founder Scott Dikkers' How to Write Funny trilogy is good. If you're starting out the first is very useful. I like the third in the series How to Write Funniest.

John Vorhaus has written several books on comedy writing, his fairly recent Little Book of Sitcom is one I keep going back to.

And, unless you're interested in becoming a stand-up, that's more or less it. Even if you're not planning to take that route I still recommend Logan Murray's Be a Great Stand Up. It's a useful insight into the minds of the dysfunctional weirdos you're likely to end up working for if you're lucky.

I've not read many comedian memoirs but Lost Voice Guy Lee Ridley's Only in It for The Parking is an inspirational read. It should be a set text for anyone moaning that they'll never make it in comedy because the odds are stacked against them.

Comedy Rules by Jonathan Lynn is full of great anecdotes plus a bunch of rules that aren't really rules. They're fascinating suggestions based on his vast experience around comedy, and he is wise and witty.

The various iterations of Alan Partridge are available in bound form. Not sure how much you learn from them, but the parodic celebrity memoir-writing skills of the Gibbons brothers make them a lot of fun.

Collections of scripts can be useful, especially of your favourite sitcoms. I have well-thumbed volumes of Seinfeld, Frasier and The Marx Brothers. For some reason I rarely have recourse to leaf through the giant slabs of paper I own featuring the complete works of Ronnie Barker, Eddie Braben and Woody Allen. Maybe it's just my personal taste, or how their works so profoundly influenced my teenage self, but somehow it feels odd to me to read their scripts rather than watch old clips.

Let's look at writing for TV in general. Blake Snyder's Save The Cat is a best-selling choice and it's easy to see why. Fun, funny, short, simple. It's aimed at movie screenwriters but so much of the advice is useful for any writer. Snyder has cleverly franchised the title with separate books for novelists, TV writers and so on. You only need to read one to pick up the essentials.

Into The Woods by John Yorke is mostly focused on TV drama, but there's so much to learn about narrative structure here that applies across all genres. Unlike most of the writers I've read on this subject, Yorke is a successful professional in the field. And unlike most of the books I've read on this subject, it's well-written.

Another writer who walks the walk is Julian Dutton, who I spoke of earlier in the chapter about visual comedy. His book Keeping Quiet: Visual Comedy in The Age of Sound is a perfect combination of history and practical help.

Before we leave the Anglosphere, I'll say a quick hello to David Crystal, an academic who has been writing about the English language for half a century. His knowledge of the written word from its thousands-year-old origins is extraordinary, and he's also a great communicator.

Many of the books are dense with facts but it's worth immersing yourself in the subject matter, as I guarantee you'll emerge with a much greater command of the language. Making Sense Of Grammar is surprisingly fun. I can't tell you how much he has improved what me do at sticking words in right order and make proper sentence.

When it comes to books on writing, fittingly the greatest book of all is called On Writing. And it's by Stephen King. No arguments on the "professional-in-the-field" front. Seriously this book is so far ahead of the competition that for me it's up there with Aristotle's Poetics as bare minimum reading requirement.

Will Storr's the Science of Storytelling is a reminder that plotting and character cannot be separated, and like Into The Woods is a gripping read.

Finally I recommend a book that has nothing to do with comedy. Or writing. Atomic Habits by James Clear teaches you how to focus on your creativity. It may seem odd and slightly weird to recommend a book that works for Bill Gates and Elon Musk. But what the heck, it works for me too and it probably will for you.

Whatever you do, however you decide to improve your writing skills, the greatest free university for British comedy writers remains the BBC.

People often talk about the BBC like it's a single entity. But the giant monster of urban myth, the wishy-washy liberal woke behemoth that rewards political correctness with overflowing vats of taxpayer's money – is actually a blob of creative matter being pulled in several directions by thousands of departments of all shapes and sizes.

Departments don't come much tinier than Radio Comedy (now swallowed up by BBC Sounds) and Children's TV.

Apart from BBC Writersroom, the tiniest of them all. If you think of kid's TV as the broom cupboard at the end of the comedy writing corridor, BBC Writersroom is inside, second shelf on the left and close to collapse.

I adore BBC Writersroom. If you do nothing else today, spend some time in the company of their website. At the top of the front page, it says "We discover, develop and champion new and experienced writing talent across the whole of the UK."

Which is exactly what they do. But even if you never get to make it onto one of their schemes, you'll find a ton of fantastic resources one click away on the website.

Want to be reminded of the basics of scriptwriting? Yes we all do, I re-watch their "scriptwriting essentials" videos all the time.

Worried about formatting? I know the answer is yes and having refused to answer this question earlier in this book, I shall send you instead to find details there.

Want to hear what the experts say? Got a question? There's a blog on every topic, by someone who understands the journey that your writing takes for every step from idea to broadcast.

You probably remember the famous advertisement "If you can read this, thank a teacher."

In this world we have a similar phrase which is "if you know how to make comedy, thank the BBC."

SUMMARY

Read.

Watch.

Learn.

40

Seven Secrets of Successful Writers

One of the great joys of writing for Horrible Histories is finding out amazing information that I would never have otherwise come across. Not all of it is useful, but recently our brilliant researcher Greg Jenner dug out a collection of the finest habits of successful writers. If you want to be effective at your work, I can guarantee that every one of these writers swore by these techniques, at least for them.

Fancy yourself as the next Charles Dickens? Follow these simple rules and the title "literary genius" will be yours. Dickens combed his hair a hundred times a day and always touched things three times for luck. In Victorian times the diagnosis of obsessive compulsive disorder did not exist, so perhaps he thought this behaviour was vital to his writing. He certainly believed the quality of his prose depended on where his bed was, and always slept facing north. When travelling he carried a compass to ensure accuracy in this.

On days when he gave public readings, Dickens had two tablespoons of rum with fresh cream for breakfast, and a pint of champagne for tea. Half an hour before the start of the reading itself, he would drink a raw egg beaten into a tumbler of sherry. If you're going to develop habits like those, I advise you to do so after you've written your first five best sellers rather than before. A cast iron constitution will help.

In a similar vein, George Orwell wrote most of 1984 in a hospital bed, with a bottle of rum hidden under the mattress. Presumably he managed to grab a few swigs when Big Sister wasn't watching.

Another vital key to your imminent success as a novelist is to eschew the bourgeois trappings of modern society, like trousers. Ernest Hemingway is rumoured to have written in the nude, standing up with his typewriter at waist level. Benjamin Franklin was also a fan of nude writing, though I gather the staff at his local library weren't so keen.

Other members of the "writing while standing" brigade included Thomas Wolfe, Lewis Carroll and Virginia Woolf. Robert Louis Stevenson, Mark Twain and Truman Capote all used to lie down when they wrote, with Capote going so far as to declare himself "a completely horizontal writer."

Woolf delighted in the physical act of writing words on paper. From the age of 11, she was continually experimenting with different kinds of pens in hope of finding one that would provide the perfect sensation. If Woolf had been around today I'm convinced that between bouts of novel writing she would have been scouring the online forums for views on how this latest version of Final Adobe Word Draft Shop 27 has made writing so much easier. It hasn't, by the way, it's merely improved the quality of your procrastination.

Agatha Christie liked to dream up plot ideas while soaking in her large Victorian bath, munching on apples. She stopped the habit when she became dissatisfied with the baths available to her. "Nowadays they don't build baths like that. I've rather given up."

According to his daughter, JD Salinger drank urine and practiced sitting in an orgone box, a device invented to restore health (It does nothing). I'd like to take his example and conclude we now have official proof that drinking urine stops you from coming up with new writing.

DH Lawrence liked to climb mulberry trees in the nude to stimulate his imagination – I bet he did, the cheeky scamp. Legendary movie maker Sam Fuller said "If a story you're writing doesn't give you a hard-on in the first couple of scenes, throw it in the god-damned garbage!" I realise this quote excludes half the population, and may not even be a writing tip, but it gives you some insight into Fuller's working habits.

If you fancy yourself as a poet, part of the key to your success will undoubtedly be to affect certain habits that will boost your profile faster than a viral clip featuring you puking outside a fashionable London nightspot. While he was a student at

Cambridge, Lord Byron bought and kept a bear, as there were no rules against such a thing in the official statutes. When the college predictably protested, Byron applied for a fellowship for the bear. Throughout his life he also kept monkeys, a crocodile and peacocks.

Tennyson liked to pretend to go to go to the toilet by dropping his trousers in front of people. I'm not sure if that was one of his habits to help him with writing, but I thought I'd share that information with you anyway.

If the nudity route is not for you, here are some sartorial secrets of success. Dr. Seuss owned hundreds of hats, in his search for inspiration he would go to his secret closet filled with hats and wear them until the words came. By the way, you're all pronouncing "Seuss" wrongly. It's supposed to rhyme with "voice", not "Zeus". Remember folks, you read that noiss here first.

Victor Hugo locked away all his formal clothes so he wasn't tempted to leave the house, wearing only a large grey knitted shawl when writing. Although if you've met even the most successful comedy writers you will know that the idea of any of them possessing formal clothing is laughable.

Hemingway, who you are already picturing standing, naked, also obsessively sharpened his pencils before writing, which I am assured is not a euphemism. Edgar Allen Poe supposedly wrote with his Siamese cat sitting on his shoulder, which makes him sound like a Bond villain.

In the days before Sudoku, Daniel Defoe liked to waste time by inventing pseudonyms for himself, using nearly 200 throughout his career. These included: Anti-King-Killer, Autho' Hubble Bubble, Count Kidney Face, Sir Fopling Tittle-Tattle, One-two-three-four and Anglipolski of Lithuania and Heliostrapolis, secretary to the Emperor of the Moon.

My favourite writing tip comes from the great French scribe Voltaire, who it is said used the naked back of his lover as a writing desk. Next time you see "I disapprove of what you say, but will defend to the death your right to say it", hold an image of where Voltaire was when he wrote that.

I hope some of these tips have been helpful. From my own experience, I've found that writing while standing, lying down, in the bath, wearing a hat or whatever, is less important than knowing what I'm writing about. If I've put the preparation in, and the work is inspiring me, I can write anywhere and in any state of attire.

I doubt if I'll ever be as renowned as any of the writers mentioned in this chapter. Maybe you won't be either.

But every morning I look forward to spending time at the most exciting place in the world, my desk. I love comedy. I love writing, and am grateful for every day that brings me a fresh opportunity to develop both. I may not sell another sitcom script or novel as long as I live. But this is what success looks like for me.

I wish you the same.

SUMMARY

Are you currently in the process of writing something you care about?

Congratulations.

You are succeeding.

Discover More About Writing Comedy

1 My website

I currently reside online at

http://davecohen.org.uk/

There you'll find blogs, courses, information and a free book to help you kick start your comedy writing. And you can sign up there for my newsletter.

2 Drop me a line

If you have any questions, email me. And I'd love to know what you thought of the book. Contact me at funnyup02@gmail.com

3 Individual coaching

If you can write, you can write comedy.

Work with me to add funny to your fiction and drama.

Want to develop your comedy career? Talk to me about adopting a professional approach.

Experienced comedy writer? Work with me on developing and rewriting your scripts.

Not sure? Drop me a line for a free initial chat funnyup02@gmail.com

4 Attend a course, or let me assess your script

I run email correspondence courses to help you write sitcom, comedy-drama, sketches and topical comedy. Check out the latest ones here:

https://www.davecohen.org.uk/learn-to-write-comedy/comedy-writing-courses/

5 Listen to our podcasts

James Cary and I have lots of new ideas lined up for our podcasts. If you'd like to sign up to our special goodies, including one-to-one script analysis, you can join our podcast crew on Patreon:

https://www.patreon.com/SitcomGeeks

You can find our 200+ podcasts on Spotify, iTunes and at the British Comedy Guide:

https://www.comedy.co.uk/podcasts/sitcom_geeks/

Testimonials

Build A Sit Com/Build A Comedy Drama

A brilliant introduction to comedy scriptwriting for novelists who want to make the switch Jessica Adams (Author Single White Email, Tom Dick and Debbie Harry; Editor Girls' Night In)

I really enjoyed Dave's course and found it very productive. Every week Dave reads and gives individual feedback on what you've done. It's like having a writing partner with tons of experience, making you face things that you might otherwise gloss over, offering constructive suggestions, and occasionally administering a small pat on the back. It's the guide, philosopher and friend of sitcom courses. William Van Dyck (Winner 2021 Pozzitive Sitcom Script Competition)

I've loved the course so far. I'm finding the specific notes on homework extremely helpful, and that they're in addition to the general notes and general instructions is really good. You're a supportive teacher and in my experience at least half of this writing game is confidence and you encourage us to push on. Fiona Faith Ross
This has been a wonderful inroad into a field I'd always wanted to enter but was never sure how to go about it. Thank you so much for all of it. James Allen

Being taken step by step, to tight time frames, has given a brilliant insight into the process and how difficult it is. If anyone was thinking of trying their hand at Sitcom writing, they would do well to try your course. Lee Dixon

Working through lockdown was the most stressful time of my career. Having this sitcom to do in down time gave me an escape, I didn't burden my family with work and the deadlines kept my mind occupied so thank you, if this course achieved nothing else it got me through covid. Steven Mucklow

Topical Comedy

It was excellent! Putting aside the credits on Breaking the News which was an unexpected bonus, I really learnt about crafting jokes and the routine of producing them. Joanne Cunningham

The course and feedback on gags has been brilliant. Uttom Chowdhury (credited on Breaking the News and The Skewer)
It was absolutely brilliant in every way. I ended up with writing credits on two shows which was a huge confidence boost and gave my writing career a valuable breakthrough. Worth the money many times over. Plus, they were super supportive and encouraging, and gave really useful expert feedback, so your gag writing will improve whatever level you're at. Fantastic and highly recommended. Alice Bright

Sketch Writing

It's been really valuable. I really understand that writing them is like practising scales to be a brilliant pianist. Having done the course, I feel much more confident about spotting a solid idea and being able to execute it all the way through to that golden second twist. It was great to be in a zoom class with like-minded people, thrashing out ideas and learning from each other's work. I highly recommend the course. Eleanor Hayward

Acknowledgments

At the risk of sounding like an Oscar-winning speech maker, I want to begin by thanking you, every blooming one of you, for supporting me over the years since this book first came out.

I love writing about comedy writing, and helping people become better writers. I couldn't have continued without your continued support. This is a scientific and financial fact.

Thanks to Dan Sweryt, who cast a clear, professional eye over the text, corrected my grammatical errors and added clarity to my jumbled thoughts on comedy writing. Dan built on the sterling work of Vivienne Riddoch, who painstakingly removed cliché and punctuation pandemonium from the original text.

I'm extremely grateful to James Cary, who has probably had as much influence on the content of this book as me. Almost everything I know about the craft of writing comedy has been learned or refined over many years in the presence of James as teacher and co-presenter of Sitcom Geeks...

...and to Pete Sinclair, who has probably made me laugh more than anyone and who since 1983 has been there for me as friend, confidante and comedy guide.

Kate my agent continues to be as helpful and supportive as ever, thanks Kate! Also to my friend Martin Bostock, who has been offering invaluable advice on the –preneur front. The brilliant designer Andy Cowles let me tap into his peerless expertise in graphic design. Julia Scheib let me get away without having to learn how to operate a computer but ended up teaching me quite a lot. Late to the party Rik Hall taught me how to format from across the Atlantic. Thank you Magic Rik. And thanks Nigel Browne for your fantastic professional guidance. Who knew running a business could be fun?

I'd like to thank Simon Nelson from BBC Writersroom for his support and advice on so much of the content, and also to Radio 4 Commissioning Editor Sioned Wiliam and Head of Radio

Comedy Julia McKenzie for their help and support. Julia has now taken over from Sioned and Richard Morris runs BBC Sounds. All miracle workers in the struggle to bring new comedy voices to the BBC. And a special personal thank you to Jon Holmes and Bill Dare, two of the best and most consistently successful radio producers. Both have been instrumental in kickstarting the careers of dozens of comedy writers.

Steven Moffat has a lovely take on the concept of "Press send", which I've adapted here with his kind permission.

Thanks to Miriam for putting up with me frequently running off "to finish writing a chapter" only to walk in on me staring goggle-eyed at the latest political developments on Twitter. And to the kids, whose influence has been profound, not least for making me laugh and keeping me up to date with what's funny. And introducing me to The Gilmore Girls, for which I will be forever grateful.

The comedy world is changing so fast we're lucky to have three websites that continue to keep pace and keep us informed. We should all be grateful to Steve Bennett at Chortle, Aaron Brown and Mark Boosey of British Comedy Guide and Bruce Dessau who runs Beyond the Joke. Plus relative newcomers The Comedy Crowd. Thanks to Jon, Omar and the gang for doing so much to encourage new writers.

There are dozens of chums from the comedy world I'd like to thank, too many to mention all but special thanks to Richie Webb, Lee Mack, Gary Delaney, Julian Dutton, Caroline Norris, Brenda Gilhooly, Neil Forsyth, Steve Doherty, Lisa Holdsworth, Daniel Peak, Paul McKenzie, Gail Renard and Nick Yapp.

Finally, thanks to the Writers' Guild of Great Britain and the Alliance of Independent Authors. Our individual skills are nothing without the help of professional bodies that look out for everyone in our wonderful but precarious profession. If you pay for nothing else, please buy membership to one or both of these small but remarkable organisations.

Stand Up, Barry Goldman
David J Cohen

"In the last anxiety-making days of lockdown David made me laugh out loud from the first few pages. This novel about the world of stand-up comedy is funnier than the real thing"
Linda Grant

"Skilfully evokes all the tension of doing your first Edinburgh Fringe but without incurring the life changing overdraft."
Jack Dee

"Powerfully funny, often moving, David has created the Jewish Adrian Mole of alternative comedy" ***David Quantick***

All I'd wanted for as long as I could remember was a woman to love, a soulmate to live with in contentment for the rest of my days: friend, lover, companion, mother to our children. Time was running out: I was getting old. Next year I would be eighteen.

Barry Goldman is a sensitive boy. He's being primed to run the family business but has discovered a talent for making audiences laugh at his silly poems.

At last, he has found something that might make him attractive to girls – in particular, Harriet Fink - but there's not much call for delicate, earnest poets in the 1970s comedy world of hot-panted dolly birds and battle-axe mothers-in-law.

Then one night he sees Kris Dean on stage and understands that the world of comedy is about to change forever.

Stand Up, Barry Goldman by David J Cohen
Available from Waterstones online
https://www.waterstones.com/book/stand-up-barry-goldman/david-j-cohen/9781999313821
Amazon books: https://www.amazon.co.uk/dp/1999313828

Printed in Great Britain
by Amazon

42716945R00139